SHIPWRECKS & SUNKEN TREASURE IN SOUTHEAST ASIA

SHIPWRECKS & SUNKEN TREASURE
IN
SOUTHEAST ASIA

TONY WELLS

TIMES EDITIONS

CONTENTS

Dedication

To all the seamen, women and children who perished in shipwrecks in the North and Southeast Asian seas throughout the ages.
You are not forgotten. God be with you all!

I also dedicate this book to my mother, grandmother, stepfather, all my relatives and friends who have supported me over the years.
I can only say I hope I have not let you down.

Acknowledgements

I would to thank the following people for their support in helping me with this book – Kim Correl, Patrick Paggeot, Johnny Tan, Jason Yoong, Sverker and Ena Hallstrom, Mike Flecker, Mike Healy, Jean-Marc Chastan, John Anderson, Tjetty, Jon McCarty, Stephane Deyrolle and Mae Tan.

From the Netherlands, my thanks to Professor Dr. J.R. Bruijn (Rijks University, Leiden), Mrs. M.C.J.C. van Hoof (General State Archives, Leiden) and Deborah van Iterson (Researcher, Leiden).

From France, thank you to Patrick Lize for proofreading and helping with research.

At the Museu De Marinha in Lisboa, I express my gratitude to Pedro Luis da Costa Gomes Lopes for helping me with Portuguese shipwreck information. A special thanks also to Portuguese researcher, Ricardo de Araujo E Melo Ribiero.

I would like to thank Jerry Caba for his support in writing the *Foreward* to this book.

I am also very grateful to Colin Sheaf (Christie's) and Edward Schneider (Christie's Images) for supplying me with excellent slides of cargoes re-covered from the *HATCHER JUNK*, the *VOC* ship *GELDERMALSEN* and the *VUNG TAU* junk.

Finally, I cannot thank Andrea Cordani (UK researcher) enough for her patience, help and research assistance for these past few months. Andrea, I owe you one!

Last, but not least, special thanks to Mr. Wong Heng, Ms. Lim Kek Hwa and all the staff at the Singapore National Library for putting up with my many requests for every imaginable book, map and microfilm in their possession.

Foreword

Most people don't know exactly what made sunken wrecks, pirates and gold or treasure stick in their minds for the very first time, or even when the first time was. It might have been going through an amusement park ride, like Pirates of the Caribbean, or reading a book from childhood, such as *Treasure Island*. It is usually impossible to say because the era of exploring far-off lands and plundering rich cargos is woven inextricably into our history.

For a wreck-hunter who dedicates time and effort into researching and finding wrecks, the enchantment of that era is potent. It's like having the chance to explore those far-away lands once again. And the more one looks for wrecks, the more one will find. This vision of the past and empathy with the people who lived then grows stronger and stronger with every cannon ball, cannon, brass divider, silver coin, jewelled cufflink, ceramic shaving mug and tortoiseshell toothbrush that is fished out of the sand.

Unfortunately, this captivation can have adverse effects on wreck hunters. The dedication to wreck-hunting can become so intense that some have become overly obsessive and guarded. Tony Wells has not fallen prey to the paranoia that can grip wreck-hunters. He is very open and his perspective has not been impaired by the riches of the sea.

As this book shows, there are plenty of shipwrecks in this region. In bringing out wealth of information on wrecks and salvage techniques, Tony hands readers a fascinating passage through history by exploring sunken wrecks and lost treasures in Southeast Asia that everyone, including the armchair treasure-hunter, can enjoy.

Gerald J. Caba
Cabaco Marine Pte Ltd
Singapore

Author's Note

To date, numerous books have been written regarding lost ships, wrecks and sunken treasures. However, the majority of these books are dedicated to North and South America, the Caribbean, South Africa and Europe. Well, that's fine but whatever happened to Southeast Asia?

For centuries, this region has been part of the great trading route from west to east, with thousands of ships traversing this route. Unless it's hidden in some deep, dark corner covered with dust, to my knowledge, not a single book yet has been written that is dedicated to shipwrecks in Southeast Asian waters. For that reason, I believe that such a book is long overdue.

This book focuses largely on Southeast Asia, which was an important part of a great shipping route that stretched from Europe and the Middle East, through India and on to China and Japan. Although the trade route from western to eastern Asia is about 2,000 years old, the wrecks discussed here date from the 16th century onwards. Many are wrecks of European powers who established colonies in Southeast Asia – the Portuguese and and Spanish who were the earliest European adventurers, followed by the Dutch and British, and trailed by the French, Swedish and Americans.

The recent discovery of wrecks such as the VOC ship *GELDERMALSEN*, the *VUNG TAU* junk, the English merchant trader *DIANA* and others has led to a greater awareness of the rich maritime history of this region and the fabulous cargo of wrecks lying on the seabed. This has led to a revived interest in salvaging wrecks.

In writing this book, I hope that Southeast Asian countries, working in conjunction with reputable salvage companies and marine archaeologists, will bring to light new and exciting finds. By cooperating, we have nothing to lose and everything to gain because these unique objects have been sitting on the seabed for centuries. The sooner we can recover these rare and precious artifacts and get them on display, whether in public museums or in private hands, the better off we will be in the end.

Tony Wells
Searchmasters (Singapore)
August 1995

1
MARITIME LEGACY

The maritime history of Southeast Asia goes back over 2,000 years. Centuries before the first Europeans even dreamed of venturing here, Southeast Asia was the meeting place of a rich and prosperous maritime trade.

After establishing booming domestic trade in the region, Southeast Asia's earliest foreign trade connections were with India and the Middle East. Although details of early trading contacts are "hidden in a dense mist", Arab and Indian traders introduced spices from the Moluccas – the original Spice Islands of Indonesia – to Europe in the fourth century A.D. It is believed that commodities from Southeast Asia were transported in phases – first by sea to India, then overland across ancient trading routes to the Middle East and ports in the Mediterranean Sea, and finally to Europe. Besides spices, Southeast Asia's wealth in other commodities also reinforced trading connections. In the first century A.D. after the Roman Emperor Vespasian prohibited the export of gold from Rome, historians believe that Indian traders turned to Southeast Asia as an alternative source of gold imports, particularly the islands of Sumatra and Java.

A 16th century map of the Orient. Lying at the crossroads of the rich trade route between the Far East and the West, Southeast Asia has attracted traders and adventurers in search of riches.

1

Besides these early Arab and Indian traders, the indigenous people of Southeast Asia, the Malays, were also traders. They have been described as *"par exellence* a sea-going people". Over the centuries, they played an important role in establishing early shipping routes east to China and west to India, the Middle East and Africa.

The Chinese also contributed to the growth in maritime trade by exporting oriental ceramics and other goods. By the beginning of the Tang dynasty in the seventh century (A.D. 618–907), ceramics were a major part of China's trade. Wares from northern China were transported overland via the famous Silk Road to as far away as Persia (modern day Iran). Goods from southern China were also shipped by sea to neighbouring Asian kingdoms, to the Middle East and North Africa by the end of the Tang period. As early as the ninth century, Chinese porcelain had reached Southeast Asia. From ports in southern China, Chinese sailing junks usually took one of two routes through Southeast Asia – they either sailed down the west coast of the Philippines, past Borneo and Sulawesi to the Moluccas Islands, or they followed the coastline of Vietnam, Thailand and the Malay peninsula with the help of monsoon winds. From there, they turned south to Java or Sumatra or headed west out to the Indian Ocean for the long journey to India and lands farther away.

It is believed that in the late 13th to early 14th century during the Vietnamese Tran dynasty (1225–1400), commercially-minded Chinese refugees fleeing from Mongol invaders settled in Vietnam and helped to trade the local ceramic wares abroad. Initially, this early trade was slow but it showed signs of expansion in the late 14th century, probably as a result of the first Ming Emperor Hong Wu's (1368–1398) attempted ban on Chinese overseas voyages. Vietnamese trade in ceramics is thought to have reached its height in the 15th and 16th centuries.

Being a region dominated by the sea, trade and shipping in Southeast Asia have been an important feature of political and economic events for centuries. Countries, kingdoms and cities have risen and fallen due to trade. These include Nagasaki in Japan, China, Tongking in North Vietnam, Annam in Central Vietnam, Cochin China in South Vietnam, Cambodia and Siam (now called Thailand). Even capital cities that were far inland like Pegu or Ava in Myanmar, Phnom Penh in Cambodia, or Ayutthaya in Siam had great river ports that were accessible to large vessels.

Among the early important trading ports of Southeast Asia were Acheh, Pasai and Kota China (all located in northern Sumatra, Indonesia), Palembang (central Sumatra), Bantam and Batavia (Java), Manilla (the Philippines) and Malacca (west coast of peninsular Malaysia). In Northeast Asia, Canton and Amoy (southern China) and Nagasaki (Japan) were the major trading ports.

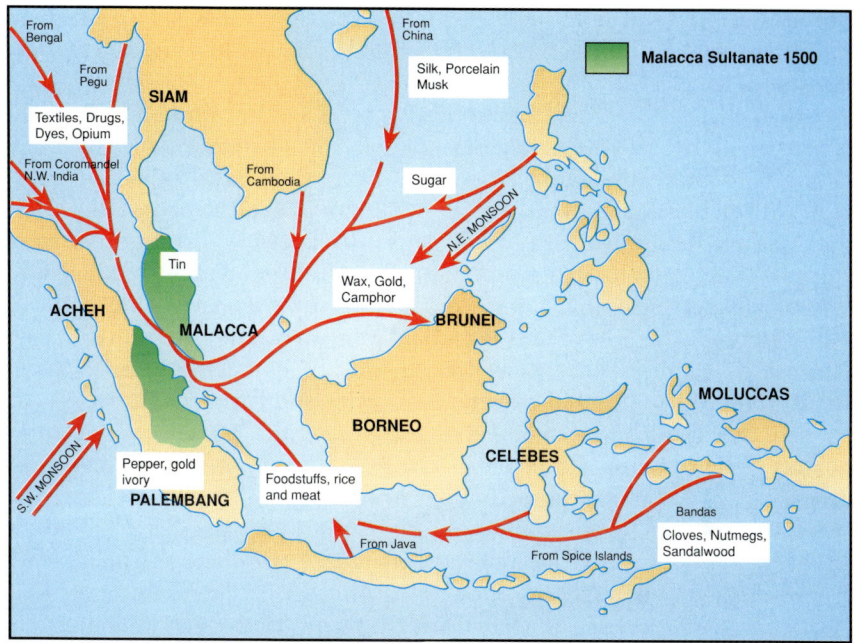

Great Trading Centers of Southeast Asia

Malacca

During the early 1500s, Malacca was believed to be the richest city in Asia. It was the main center of trade in Southeast Asia at the time. Its harbour was filled with ships from all over Northeast and Southeast Asia, as well as with vessels from as far away as Arabia, India and Africa. Merchants came to trade and barter goods of every imaginable kind – ivory, oriental ceramics, gold, precious stones, perfumes and spices. Just about every type of luxury and exotic merchandise was traded here.

The *Sejarah Melayu* (the Malay Annals which contain a record of Malay history going back 700 years) describes Malacca as follows:

> *"All the trade from the lands above the wind and from the lands below the wind came to Malacca; crowded with people was the city of Malacca at that time. The Arabs called it malakat, which means the collecting centre for commerce, because all kinds of goods were found there ..."*

The arrival of the Europeans to Southeast Asia was inevitable as news of Malacca's wealth, the need for spices and the many untapped treasures of the Orient was too much for European adventurers to resist. The Portuguese, already established in India and not wanting to miss out on Malacca's prosperity, sent a fleet of five Portuguese ships to Malacca under the command of Captain Diego Lopes de Sequeira. They arrived in Malacca harbour on September 11, 1509. Sequeira's mission was to set up a trading post there and further establish strongholds for the growing Portuguese empire in the East.

All went well at first, but the Portuguese, being unfamiliar with the Malay customs, unknowingly offended the local people when Captain Sequeira handed Bendehara Tun Mutahir (the chief minister) a gold necklace with his left hand. This was a tremendous insult to the Malays. The local people devised a plan to kill the Portuguese. Sequeira got word of this plan but it was too late to save several of his men who were killed and taken prisoner. Sequeira himself escaped by quickly launching his ship and sailing for the port of Goa in India. Upon arrival at Goa, Sequeira told Alfonso de Albuquerque (then the Viceroy of Portuguese territories in India, 1509–1515) of the ill treatment, murder and capture of his men.

Albuquerque armed several vessels and prepared for war. A fleet of 18 vessels departed Goa for Malacca. On July 1, 1511, the Portuguese fleet arrived at Malacca and immediately fired their cannons to display their strength. Later the same day, Albuquerque dispatched a letter to Malacca's sultan demanding the release of the Portuguese men held prisoner. After a few days of negotiations, they were released on the condition that Albuquerque would not attack the city. But a few days later, Albuquerque broke his promise. After nine days of fierce fighting which led to many casualties on both sides, the Portuguese took control of Malacca. The sultan managed to escape certain death by fleeing into the dense jungle with his family and surviving followers. He later set up a new capital in Johor at the southern end of the Malay peninsula.

Eighteenth century Dutch bronze cannon on display in modern day Malacca. The Dutch were colonial masters of Malacca for 183 years, from 1641 to 1824, until the British took over.

THE LURE OF THE SPICE TRADE

What lured the early Europeans to the East Indies? The answer simply is spices.

Although spices were available in Mediterranean ports such as Constantinople and Cairo, by the time they reached Europe, they had passed through a number of middlemen and traders, thus pushing up prices. In 15th and 16th century Europe, the Portuguese and the Spanish, who were the most adventurous explorers and navigators of their time, determined to go directly to the source of these spices and set out in search of the fabled riches of the Spice Islands.

Among the most valuable spices were cloves and nutmeg which fetched vast amounts of money. Nutmeg and cloves originated in the Moluccas – a group of islands in the Indonesian archipelago that became known as the Spice islands. Pepper was grown in the islands of Sumatra and Java. During the Middle Ages in Europe, pepper was such a prized commodity that it was even used as a mode of payment. In some parts of Europe, it was used to pay rent, and this is how the phrase "peppercorn rent" came about.

Every European power that came to Asia in search of trade competed for a share of the lucrative trade in spices. The Portuguese were the first to capture control of the Spice Islands and fended off the Spanish. However, they were later driven out by Dutch colonial ambitions in the Indonesian islands. The British also tried to gain a foothold but faced opposition from the Dutch.

The once prosperous and flourishing port of Malacca became almost a ghost town after the Portuguese conquest as trade was disrupted. Declining trade was also brought about by the high duties imposed on Muslim traders and the chaotic conditions resulting from many expeditions and wars against the Portuguese. The struggle for political power between the Portuguese, Johor and Acheh after 1511 contributed to Malacca's failing political dominance. There were many expeditions sent from Johor Lama (the capital of Johor, located several kilometers up the Johor River) by the ousted Malacca sultan to recapture his former town. The Dutch and Achinese also sent several war fleets to Malacca separately to drive out the Portuguese. Finally, the Dutch succeeded in taking Malacca in 1641.

Acheh

By the 16th century, the port of Acheh in northern Sumatra had replaced Malacca in trading importance. Being strategically located at the northern entrance of the Straits of Malacca also enabled Acheh to control the passage of ships into the archipelago. The Achinese wanted to break the Portuguese monopoly of trade in Southeast Asia and declared war on them in Malacca between 1529 and 1587. Major offensives were conducted in 1537, 1548, 1568, 1570 and 1574–75. These attacks weakened the Portuguese and contributed to shortening their colonial rule in Malacca.

Acheh's main exports were pepper, spices, gold, camphor and rice. It also had trade relations with China, especially after 1519. This is probably because in that year, relations between China and Portugal were severed as a result of the arrogant Portuguese attitude at a meeting on the Pearl River in China. Records after 1519 indicate that as many as 18 to 20 ships loaded with pepper sailed from Acheh to China annually.

Achinese trade covered a wide area, stretching as far as Egypt in the west and China in the east. Westward ports included India, Ceylon (present day Sri Lanka), and the Red Sea. Achinese trade voyages also covered the coastal states of western Sumatra, the Malay peninsula and China.

Bantam, the Spice Islands and Batavia

Between 1569 and 1610, Bantam in western Java was the most important port for the pepper trade. Upon arrival at the port of Bantam, a Dutchman known as Van Leur wrote this lively description (extracted from K.R. Haellquist, *Asian Trade Routes, Continental and Maritime*):

> "On 22 June 1596, after a long and unlucky passage around the Cape of Good Hope and northeast across the Indian Ocean, the four Amsterdam ships of the first Dutch 'Company for Afar' came to anchor before the Javanese town of Bantam, thus ending a voyage that begun on 21 March 1595 ... the accounts of the first voyage transport us into the mist of everyday life in the town of Bantam – ceremonial visits are exchanged with the town authorities, the governor and the shahbandar; nobles and merchants come on board. There came such a multitude of Javanese and other nations, such as Turks, Chinese, Bengali, Arabs, Persians, Gujerati and others that one could hardly move ... they came so abundantly that each nation took a spot on the ships where they displayed their goods, the same as if it were on a market."

The first Dutch trade expedition to arrive in Indonesia, led by Cornelius de Houtman (1595–97), was well received in Bantam by the local ruler. The second expedition (1597–99) was led by Jacob van Neck. Both expeditions were successful in establishing trade relations with the local leaders and the vessels returned to the Netherlands fully laden with spices and other goods.

The Dutch were on good terms with the rulers of Bantam until the Sultan insisted on trading with other Europeans, namely the British, who were allowed to set up a factory on Bantam in 1610. Hostilities began and the Dutch retaliated by blockading Bantam for a period of 10 years (1618–28), effectively destroying Bantam's trade.

As the spice trade was a major economic concern, it was important for the Dutch to control the territories that produced the spices. Ambon Island (located just south of Ceram Island in Indonesia) was one of the first to come under their control in 1600. Steven van der Hagen, the Dutch envoy to the East, concluded a treaty with the Sultan of Ambon that gave the Dutch monopoly over the local spice trade but this was strongly opposed by the Portuguese who were already established on the island. In 1605, the Dutch gained control of Ambon by force. Soon afterwards, they gained control over Ternate (1608) and later Banda (1609).

In 1619, Jakarta (in western Java) became the main Dutch trading port in the East. The Dutch then renamed it Batavia. The British and Portuguese were forced out from the other islands and by 1669, the Dutch had total control over almost all the Indonesian islands and were able to monopolize the spice trade in the region.

Manilla

The Spanish colonized the Philippines in order to compete with the Portuguese for a share of the spice trade. In the year 1519, a fleet of Spanish ships led by Ferdinand Magellan headed eastward until they arrived in the Philippines. Unfortunately, due to a misunderstanding with some of the local rulers, Magellan was killed but the route to the Philippines was established. However, it was not until 1570 that a peace treaty was signed between Spain and a local Philippine chieftain. Shortly afterwards, hostility between the Filipinos and the Spanish was sparked off by an accidental firing of a Spanish cannon which led to rebellions and fighting, and eventually, the Philippines was captured by the Spanish. In 1571, the Spanish settlement was moved from Panay to Manilla.

Spain soon took control of the neighbouring islands of Visayas, Mindoro and Catanduanes. By 1574, most of the islands of the Philippines were successfully established under Spanish rule with Manilla as the main base and port.

The Spaniards ruled over the Philippines and controlled all incoming and outgoing trade which was the major source of revenue. Large quantities of silver were shipped on galleons from Acapulco, Mexico (which had also been colonized by the Spanish) to Manilla, resulting in the "Manilla galleon" trade. The king of Spain only allowed the galleon trade to take place between Acapulco and Manilla. Silver from Acapulco was then shipped directly to Cadiz, Spain where it was traded for other goods. Other major exports from the Philippines were textiles, pottery, perfumes, and spices but this trade declined in the 17th century when the Spanish began to trade with the Americas and English merchants.

In 1810, Mexican nationalists began a revolt against Spain that eventually led to the creation of the Republic of Mexico and the end of the Manilla galleon trade in 1815. With no revenue from the silver trade, the Spaniards had no choice but to look to other alternatives in the Philippines. They introduced new crops such as sugarcane, tobacco, cotton and indigo (for dyes) and opened up Manilla to international trade.

Ships trading at the port of Batavia in Java in the 18th century.

European Expansion Along the Spice Route

In 1498, Vasco da Gama made the first successful voyage round the Cape of Good Hope, sailing from Europe to India. This journey opened up more than just a sea route to the east; it also led to the eventual political and economic domination of Southeast Asia by the Europeans. The Portuguese were the first Europeans to sail to the East and establish trading posts in Asia. Other Europeans – the Spanish, Dutch, English, Swedish, and French – soon followed in the Portuguese wake towards the riches of the East.

The success of early trade missions sent from Europe to the East led to the formation of trading companies. The *Vereenigde Oost-Indische Compagnie* (VOC) or the United East India Company was established in 1602 to handle trade between the Netherlands and territories east of the Indian Ocean. On December 31, 1600, the Company of Merchants of London trading in the East Indies, otherwise known as the English East India Company (EIC), received its royal charter to sail east and establish trade.

Southeast Asia
Many of the small and strategically located ports and trading centers were muscled out of local hands and placed under European rule. For instance, in 1605, the Dutch gained control of Ambon by force. They then attacked

and acquired Tidore (southeast of Ternate) in May 1605. In 1608 and 1609 respectively, the Sultan of Ternate and ruler of Banda island were forced into a treaty under which they had to accept Dutch sovereignty and grant the Dutch monopoly of the spice trade for their protection. Similarly the islands of Lonthrop, Run and Ceram were forced to conclude such "treaties" with the Dutch. When the ruler of Macassar refused to bow to the Dutch, the Dutch used their military power and Macassar was defeated in 1667. The Dutch ruled over these islands with an iron fist, suppressing uncooperative local leaders. The ports of Bantam and Batavia were soon dominated by the Dutch. In the Philippines, the Spanish also used similar tactics to control the local rulers.

After establishing a factory at Bantam in 1610 much to the protest of the Dutch, the English East India Company were then more prepared to face fierce competition from the Portuguese and the VOC for a share of trade in Southeast Asia. Expansion was the key. In 1651, the EIC established a factory at Hoogly in Bengal, India. This factory was abandoned in 1685 when they opened a pepper plantation at Bengkulu (western Sumatra).

With the outbreak of the French Revolution in 1789, revolutionary ideas spread throughout Europe. A rebellion in Holland against the Dutch monarchy in 1793 forced King William V to flee to England in 1795. A treaty was concluded between King William V and Britain in 1788 to prevent the fall of Dutch colonial lands into local hands. Thus, the British occupied Malacca (1795), South Africa and Ceylon (1796), the Spice Islands (1801) and Java (1811). After the end of the Napoleonic Wars, Java and Malacca were returned to the Dutch in 1816.

British interests in the region increased with the acquisition of Penang in 1785 and in Singapore in 1819. Noting its strategic location at the southern tip of peninsular Malaysia, the once sleepy island of Singapore soon became a very prosperous trading port and still remains so to this day. During the later half of the 19th century, many Malay states came under increasing British influence. Meanwhile, the British were also firmly entrenched in India and Burma.

Northeast Asia
The first Europeans to reach the shores of Japan around 1543 were Portuguese sailors. For almost a century, the Portuguese carried out trade relations with Japan. Their sailing route carried them from Lisbon to the Japanese port of Nagasaki via Goa, Malacca and Macau. This long sea route from Portugal to Japan took at least two years and four months.

The Dutch began trading with Japan in July 1609 when two Dutch ships, *ROODE LEEUW MET PIJLEN* and *GRIFFIOEN*, entered the port of the island of Hirado (off western Kyushu) to establish trade relations. Two months later, the Dutch delegates received a guarantee of unimpeded trade and the right to abode in Japan. A depot was opened for the VOC in Hirado and was in use until 1641 when it was moved to Nagasaki.

In Taiwan (then known as Formosa), the VOC built Fort Zeelandia in 1624 which became its strategic base and commercial center for northern Asia. Occupation of Formosa enabled the Dutch to benefit from prosperous trade between China and Japan.

The EIC also established a factory at Japan on December 3, 1613, but it was abandoned 10 years later due to problems caused by Dutch superiority and company profit losses.

Although the ports of China were officially opened to foreign trade in 1684, European trade at Whampoa (Canton) did not begin until 1699. The port of Amoy, profiting from English voyages there in the 1670s and the early 1680s, attracted nine vessels. However, determined efforts by the EIC and the accommodating attitude of the local officials and merchants soon reversed the trend in Canton's favour.

A period of intense rivalry between the ports of Amoy, Ningpo (Tinghai on Chusan Island), and Canton for European business ensued for five years. Seven, twelve and eight ships respectively called in at these ports in the 1690s. In 1703, the EIC concluded that Canton was a preferable port to the others because it had quicker dispatch and cheaper prices. By 1705, most ships were directed to Canton.

The period between 1685 and 1730 was the heyday of the junk trade. Although the EIC established direct trade links with China around the turn of the century (1700s), the VOC preferred to be served by Chinese shipping (see illustration of Chinese junk below). But problems with quality control of Chinaware and tea ordered via Chinese *nachodas* (purchasers) who visited Batavia forced the Dutch to new initiatives. When the EIC established a direct link to Canton in 1727, the Dutch governor-general in Batavia feared that the EIC direct participation would reduce the trade traffic between the Indies and China. VOC records show that this fear was confirmed – the blow to Chinese shipping led to a steady decrease in the junk trade at Batavia.

Aside from precious metals, the EIC's exports to Asia included woollen textiles, broadcloth (a woollen textile that derived its name from its width of one-and-a quarter yards), unwrought metals such as iron, lead, tin, copper, quicksilver (mercury), as well as luxury goods such as corals, ivory, swords, sporting guns and assorted *object d'art*.

The 18th century saw a great development in the Europe to China cotton trade. In the later part of the century, the EIC sent four or five ships to China every year but the major part of the cotton was carried there in country ships. This cotton trade increased so greatly that no less than 40 EIC ships went to Canton in the year 1789. Other European and American vessels later participated heavily in this cotton trade.

During the 17th century, the Dutch considered porcelain and silks to be the most important Chinese merchandise. However, by the end of the century, tea was in great demand in Europe. In those days, China was the only country in the world where tea was grown in such large quantities. Chinese junks laden with tea ferried back and forth to Batavia. Foreign ships were allowed only into Canton but were not allowed to sell any of their goods. The purchased tea had to be paid for in silver on the spot.

It was the China tea trade that brought in the clipper – the sailing ship in which speed mattered above everything. The quicker the ships could complete their homeward voyages to Europe or America, the faster they could return to China, load up and set sail again.

Fortunately for the Europeans and Americans, the Chinese had a passion for opium. A huge illegal traffic in opium developed, with opium produced in India being smuggled into China. When the Opium Wars (1839–1842) between England and China ended in China's defeat, China opened five ports to free foreign trade – Canton, Amoy, Foochow, Ningpo and Shanghai. Britain was given control of Hong Kong island and so the China market was open to merchants from the West.

The Commercial Attractions of the East

Maritime trade in Southeast Asia, which began as a small scale localized trading, attracted merchants and traders from all over the world. It grew to phenomenal heights by the 17th century despite the dangers of sea travel and the great distances involved. Merchants and mariners were drawn to the spices, silk, precious stones, ceramics and tea of the Far East.

European trade caused many Asian ports to prosper – Ternate, Penang, Bantam, Batavia, Canton, Nagasaki, Manilla and Saigon are a few such examples. These ports had already been trading goods on a small scale with their neighbouring countries for years. However, with the arrival of the Europeans and then later the Americans, their trade escalated to phenomenal heights. Homeward-bound ships headed for the West were heavily laden with spices, porcelain, ceramics, gold, Nanking silks, opium, tea, ivory and other commodities that were in demand. This trade was very lucrative – profits often amounted to 100% or more on oriental goods shipped back to Europe and America.

By the 19th century, merchant ships from the West were trading at virtually every port in Southeast Asia. By this time, however, the sailing era of junks, galleons, clippers and opium runners had come to an end with the advent of steam-powered ships.

SAILING SHIPS THROUGH THE CENTURIES

ADMIRAL
The commanding officer of a fleet of ships. Can also refer to the lead ship in a fleet.

BARK (BARQUE)
Square-rigged sailing ship with three masts.

BLOCKADE-RUNNER
Ship that tries to go through a blockaded port.

BRIG
Square-rigged ship with two masts.

BRIGANTINE
Two-masted ship with a square-rigged foremast and a fore-and-aft rigged mainmast.

BURTHEN
Refers to the carrying capacity of a ship.

CARAVEL
Small, light sailing ship that was the favourite ship of Spanish and Portuguese explorers between the 15th to 17th centuries. The early caravels were small, between 35 and 90 tons, although some later Portuguese ships were twice this size. By 1575, caravels were scarcely used, losing out to the heavier naos as transport and to the faster pataches as dispatch carriers.

CARRACK (*see picture above*)
A common large European merchant ship in the 16th and 17th centuries. It had a high forecastle and was usually square-

rigged on the fore- and mainmast and lateen-rigged on the mizzen mast. This vessel was commonly used as an early freighter by the Portuguese and Dutch for long cargo and passenger hauls between Europe and the East Indies on voyages that took from six to 18 months. It had a cargo capacity of up to 1,500 tons or more and could accommodate 1,000 passengers and crew. Between 1550 and 1650, they were replaced by the naos.

CLIPPER
Very fast and sleek 19th century sailing ship made popular by the Americans. They had slender hulls and tall masts. Were increasingly replaced by steamships after the 1870s.

CORVETTE
This vessel was in use around 1800 as a light warship and scout. It was built along the lines of a frigate but was much smaller, carrying about 20 10-caliber guns. Spanish corvettes sometimes carried treasure.

DESTROYER
Fast light warship developed in the late 19th century.

DHOW
Small lateen-rigged sailing ship that was commonly used in the Indian ocean. It was common among Asian traders, especially the Arabs.

EAST INDIAMEN
Sailing ships of the English, Dutch, Portuguese or other European nations that traded in Southeast Asia and the Far East. By the 18th century, these sailing ships dominated maritime trade in the region.

FORECASTLE
The raised or upper deck at the front of a ship. Was used by artillery.

FOREMAST
The mast nearest to the bow or front of the ship.

FRIGATE
Small warship that was fast and easily manoeuvred. Its development began in the 1580s and was in action in all European fleets by 1640. It varied in size from 900 to 1,700 tons and carried between 36 and 72 cannons and carronades. From 1700 onwards, these vessels were frequently used to carry large treasure shipments.

GALERA
Spanish warship constructed along the same lines as galleys.

GALLEON (*see picture below*) and NAO
These were large sailing ships developed around the 16th century from the carrack but with a lower forecastle. They were used initially as warships but were later also used for trading purposes. The galleon and nao were identical in construction and differed only in name and in the armaments carried. The galleon was a heavily armed fighting ship which was

usually prohibited from carrying cargo except registry treasure. The nao was the transport and freighter ship with few guns that was escorted by the galleons. From 1550 to 1600, the typical galleon and nao ranged in size from 300 to 600 tons, with exceptionally large ones reaching 1,000 tons. In 1590, for instance, a 400-tonner was 103 feet long, with a 32-foot beam and a 20-foot draft. Its armament was 8 bronze and 4 iron cannons and 24 bronze or iron versos.

GALLEY
A warship powered by both sails and oars.

GROSS TONNAGE
Cubic capacity or volume of a ship's space below deck. It is calculated in cubic feet divided by one hundred.

JUNK
A sailing vessel found in the Far East that was particularly used by the Chinese. It was characterized by a flat bottom, high stern and square bow.

LATEEN-RIGGED
Triangular-shaped fore-and-aft sails on a ship.

LONGBOAT
The largest boat carried on board a ship.

LORCHA
Light sailing ship with a Western-style hull but whose sails are rigged like a Chinese junk.

MAIL SHIP
Used to carry public mail and packages in the 19th century.

MAINMAST
The largest or main mast on a sailing ship closest to the bow or front of the ship.

MIZZEN MAST
The third mast on a sailing ship.

PACKET BOAT
A boat that travelled on a regular route carrying mail and freight between ports. Sometimes also carried passengers.

PADDLEWHEEL STEAMER
Vessels driven by paddlewheels instead of sails. After the opening the Suez Canal in 1869, they gained dominance over sailing ships.

PIRATE
Persons or a ship that robs and plunders other ships on the sea.

PROA (PERAHU)
Southeast Asian sailing boat with lateen-rigged sails found in the Malay archipelago and the Indonesian islands.

PRIVATEER
Person or ship licensed by the government to carry out hostilities against enemy merchant shipping. This can also refer to the ship itself.

QUARTERDECK
Part of the upper deck at the ship's stern.

REGISTER SHIP
Term used to describe ships carrying treasure such as the Spanish Manilla galleon that transported treasure from the Americas to Spain.

ROADS
Area of water just outside a main harbour where ships can anchor.

ROADSTEAD
The entrance to a harbour.

SAMPAN
Small boat widely used in the Far East and Southeast Asia with oars or paddles as well as sails.

SCHOONER
Sailing vessel introduced in the early 18th century, usually with two masts carrying fore-and-aft sails and topsails on the fore-mast.

SKIFF
Small, light open boat with one or two sets of oars as well as a sail.

SLOOP
Small sailing boat with fore-and-aft rigging on a single mast.

SNOW
Two-masted merchant ships like a brig common among the Europeans between the 16th and 19th centuries.

SQUARE-RIGGED
A ship rigged with square-shaped sails.

STEAMER
Ship propelled by steam-generated power. Steamers replaced sailing ships by the end of the 1800s.

STERN
The rear end of a ship.

TRANSPORT
Ship that carried military troops.

A sailing vessel in Indonesia in the 1800s.

COINS AND CURRENCY

While some of the currency and coinage discussed here were used in Southeast Asia, other European coinage is also explained for the reader to have a better appreciation of the value of cargoes shipped.

Bastardo
Portuguese tin coin introduced by Alfonso de Albuquerque in Malacca in 1511.

Bonk
A name given to the rectangular coins struck in Java by the Dutch from 1796 to 1818. Bonks varied in size from a one-half *stuiver* to eight *stuivers*.

Top: Islamic tin tokens from Malacca
(1408–1511)
Middle: Portuguese bastardo (1511–21)
Bottom: VOC tin stuiver (1778–1781)

Cob money
A term applied to early Mexican and South American money, both in gold and silver, from the method of striking the coins with a hammer.

Coroa / crown
A gold coin of Portugal of the value of 5,000 *reis*. It was first issued in 1835. There is a half and fifth *coroa*.

Crown (gold)
An English gold coin first issued in November 1556, originally called a crown or Double Rose. It was current for five shillings and was made of 22-carat gold fine. The French gold version issued in the 16th century was known as *Couronne du Solein*. It was of the same weight and quality as the English Crown of the Rose issued in the reign of Henry VIII.

Crown (silver)
The English silver coin of this denomination was first issued in 1551.

Cruzado
Also called *crusado* and *crusade*, this is a solid gold coin of Portugal initially issued in 1438. The value of the *cruzado* was originally 390 *reis*, and in 1517 it was fixed at four *tostoes* or 400 *reis* (that is, the tenth part of the *moidore*). In 1688, a *Cruzado Nuevo*, also called *pinto*, was issued. It had a value of 480 *reis*.

Ducat
Also called *ducato* and *dukat*. The best known of European gold coins. Generally supposed to have been first issued in 1150. The *ducat* was extensively copied by the chief rulers of Europe. There are divisions as low as 32nd and multiples as high as pieces of over 100 *ducats*. It also occurs in square and hexagonal shapes.

Duit
Also variously written *duyt*, *dute* and *doit*, this is a copper coin to the value of one-eighth of a *stuiver*. It was issued in various provinces of the Low Countries from

about 1580 to the beginning of the 19th century. The Dutch government also issued *duits* in copper and lead for their possessions in Ceylon from 1782 to 1792, and for Java from 1764 to the early part of the 19th century.

Escudo

The term *Escudo de Oro* is generally applied to the gold ducat type issued in the beginning of the 16th century, the value appeared to have been one-eighth of a doubloon. In the silver series, there was also an *escudo* of five *pesetas* issued for Tarragona in 1809 and another for Lerida of the same date. Silver *escudo* were also extensively struck during the Spanish occupation of the Low Countries. It had a value of ten *reals* (1864). The *escudo* was also a gold coin of Portugal originally issued about 1720 with a value of 1600 *reis*, which receives its name from the large shield on the reverse.

Florin (gold)

The gold *florin* was first coined in the Republic of Florence in 1252. The obverse bore a full-length figure of St. John the Baptist with the legend S. IOANNES. B. (Sanctus Johannes Baptisa). On the reverse was a lily with the arms of the city of Florence and the inscription FLORENTIA, usually preceded by a small cross. In England, the gold florin was first issued by Edward III in 1343 for Aquitaine. Its weight was 108 grains and 23 carats. The gold florin was also extensively copied in Spain, the Low Countries and especially Hungary and Germany.

Florin (silver)

The silver *florin* or *fiorino d'argento* of

Florence was introduced about the same time as the gold *florin*, its value being one-tenth of the latter. It bore the rhyming Latin verse, *"Det tibi florer / Christus, Florentia, vere"*. The Dutch guilder or florin contained 20 *stuivers* and may be regarded as equivalent of the English florin. The expression "a ton of gold" which often occurs in Dutch records merely means 100,000 guilders worth of anything. Silver *florins* or two-shilling pieces were also issued in England in 1849.

Guilder

Two-and-a-half *guilders* were equal to one *rijksdaaler*. The *guilder* is divided into 100 cents. It weighs 154.32 grains. Of the Dutch gold coins, the largest is the 10 *guilder* piece, sometimes called the *florin*, which weighs 103.7 grains.

Sycee silver

The name sycee from the Cantonese *Hsi Ssu* means "fine floss silk" and it is given to these ingots, alluding to the purity of the metal. It is run into circular or shoe-shaped ingots called *schuyt* or "boats" in the Dutch East Indies and bears an inscription or stamp on its upper surface. The standard ingot weighs about 50 *taels* though smaller ones were also made. All ingots or shoes, however, are not of such pure silver or "touch". (see *Ting* and *Yuan Pao* below.)

Gold coin from Johor dated between 1722 to 1760.

Kijang

A gold coin from Kelantan (Malaysia) believed to have been issued from the 1400s onwards. Because of its animal inscription of a bull (*kijang*) on the obverse, it was also referred to as the Barking Deer coin. Jawi inscriptions appear on the reverse of all *kijang* coins whose average weight was from 0.6 to 0.7 grams. *Kijang* coins were widely circulated in the northern Malay states of Kelantan, Trengganu, Pahang, Kedah, Perak and the southern Thai provinces of Patani, Jala and Saiburi.

Peso

The Spanish equivalent of the dollar. It primarily means weight and, by implication, the weight of an ounce. The *peso* at times had a value of 10 *reals*. It was also frequently called the *piastre*.

Real

A silver coin that was first issued in Spain in 1350 and originally called *nummus realis* or "money of the king" from which *real* was abbreviated. It was one-eighth of the *peso* and was divided into 34 *maravedis* or eight-and-a-half *cuartos*. When the East India Company was chartered in 1600, it struck a silver crown, half-crown, shilling and sixpence for use in India. These were also known as eight *reals*, four *reals*, two *reals* and a *real*.

Rijder

The silver *rijder* or *rijderdaaler* was originally issued in 1581. This coin is sometimes referred to as the *ducaton*, and it was usually computed at 40 *stuivers*.

Rijksdaaler

Also known as *Rix Daler*. The Dutch equivalent of the *reichsthaler*. It was is-

sued by the Dutch early in the 16th century.

Sovereign

A large gold coin to the value of 20 shillings issued in England in 1489. It was also frequently called the Double Rose, being twice the weight and value of the Pose Nobel. Sovereigns struck in 1817 had a value of 20 shillings (one pound). Double sovereigns were struck from 1823 to 1826 and a five sovereign or five-pound piece appeared in 1887.

Spie

A slang term for the copper one-cent coin of the Netherlands.

Thaler

The best known of all the coins of the European continent. The Spanish silver *thaler* was valued at one-fourth of a *ducat*. For Germany in the 1600s, it was 90 *kreuzer* or one-and-a-half *gulden*. It was also issued in gold.

Ting

The former name for the silver ingots or shoes of China. The more modern word is *pao*. The word *ting* generally refers to the ingot weighing 50 taels. Another name for this is *yin ting*.

Chinese bronze money.

Yuan Pao

These words have been used as a name for Chinese paper money and silver ingots. It was also the Chinese name for "original coin".

2
WHY DID THE SHIPS SINK?

For thousands of years, sea transportation was the only practical means of getting people and goods from one place to another. Thousands of ships of all origins have passed through Southeast Asian waters over the centuries, transporting cargoes of every imaginable variety.

In view of the tremendous volume of trade that took place in Southeast Asia and the numerous disputes between the colonial powers and local rulers, it is not surprising that many wrecks are found in Southeast Asian waters today. Actual examples of shipwrecks are found in Chapter 6.

Dangerous reefs

Of the thousands of passing ships, many hundreds were wrecked on hidden or un-charted reefs. In the early days, when a ship was wrecked on a reef or shoal, the survivors, if any, upon returning to port would immediately report the reef's position to map-makers or cartographers (the equivalent of today's hydrographic

A wrecked galleon lies beached on a sandbank.

society). The reef's position would then be marked on the latest nautical charts, hopefully preventing other ships from being wrecked at the same place. Those were the days of the pioneers – the days of trial and error – at the time, there was no other way.

Ironically, vessels that were employed for the purpose of hydrographic surveying have on occasion also been wrecked while surveying despite having the most cautious of captains on board. The crew of these ships had to take depth soundings within minutes of each other and constantly monitored the soundings to map the sea bed. In 1789, the VANSITTART, an EIC surveying vessel had almost completed its survey of the Gaspar Straits in Indonesia with everything was going well when suddenly it hit a shoal, making the ship a *victim* of the very thing that it was employed to prevent! It just goes to show that it could happen to anyone at any time.

During the early 18th century, some of these known dangerous reefs had floating buoys anchored upon them to warn approaching vessels of their presence. However, at times, these buoys were more deceptive than helpful. When approaching a dangerous area, some captains depended

THE EARLY CARTOGRAPHERS

The Dutch were particularly good at charting places and publishing their results in nautical maps and navigation manuals. In 1584, Lucas Janszoon Wagenaer published *Spieghel der Zeevaert*, a two-volume folio collection of charts engraved on copper plates depicting the West European continental coast from the North Cape to Cadiz, Spain and accompanied by the relevant sailing directions.

This work was later translated into English in the Armada year (16th century) under the title of *The Mariner's Mirror*. It was such a great improvement from the few sailing directions previously published that it long remained the model for all future productions of this kind, which were called *waggoners* in England until far into the 18th century. Wagenaer's *Spieghel* was the first book to print standardized symbols for buoys, sea-marks, safe anchorages and hidden and dangerous rocks. Though the Spaniards had begun to engrave and publish nautical charts a few years before the appearance of those in the *Spieghel der Zeevaert*, the latter became widely used among mariners. However, early in the 18th century, both the English and the French surpassed the Dutch in the production of accurate globes, maps and charts.

totally on the marker buoys, unaware of the possibility that a previous storm may have relocated or washed the buoys away. And by the time they realized this, they were sometimes shipwreck victims themselves!

Wars

Wars also played their part in the wrecking of ships. Besides the obvious cause of being sunk by cannon fire in the heat of battle, some ship captains on being chased, being underarmed, outnumbered or simply having a smaller or faster vessel, might decide to try and outrun the pursuing ships. Being in uncharted waters, the captain would not have had time to take depth soundings or send a smaller boat out ahead for the same purpose, therefore putting the ship and its crew in jeopardy. Under these circumstances, it is easy to understand that the captain might not have much choice at the time. Sometimes the ship being pursued might run up on a reef or shoal, but in other instances, the captain might be lucky enough to have a shallower draft enabling his vessel to just clear the reef while the pursuing ship might not be so lucky.

Weather

Weather is always a major consideration in sea travel. Again, I am not only referring to obvious weather hazards such as typhoons, rough seas and heavy gales. In fact, cloudy weather was the reason for the wrecking of quite a number of vessels.

Positioning or rather the lack of it was a dangerous situation. In the early days of sailing with the aid of instruments, the sun was used to determine latitude and longitude. Latitude positions were taken by the sailors throughout the decades with instruments such as astrolabes, cross-staffs (a universal horologe for finding the hour of the day in every latitude), cellestial/terrestrial globes, calendars, chronometers and sextants. If the weather was cloudy, the captain and/or pilot had no way of knowing the ship's location. Sometimes, the weather was cloudy for days or even weeks at a time. In this case, they would simply steer by their compass, drop their log-screw (speed indicator) overboard and guess or estimate the distance they had travelled so far. Combined with prevailing winds and changing currents, they sometimes ended up a few hundred miles off course and sometimes were shipwrecked.

When the ship was near a dangerous area and the captain was unable to determine the exact position due to the overcast sky, there was nothing to do but hope. At best, the captain could place his best lookout up in the crows nest, looking for any breakers or discoloured water that indicated a dangerous shallow reef or shoal ahead. But it is hard enough to spot breakers and discoloured water on sunny days, let alone on a cloudy day.

Even on good days, the real difficulty was to ascertain their longitude accurately. Longitude was estimated from the meridian of Saint Michael, one of the islands in the Azores off the coast of Spain, on the grounds that compass readings were most accurate there and least distorted by magnetic interference. It was not until the chronometer was invented in the latter half of the 18th century that this difficulty was overcome.

Lightning also brought several seaman and ships to their doom. During thunderstorms, the mast of sailing ships acted as magnets to lightning. In the book, *The Old Country Trade of the Indies* by W.H. Coates, one account concerning an English East Indiaman struck by lightning said:

"On this same day, while the storm was so severe, a strange thing happened. Three thunderbolts struck our vessel. The first fell on the foremast, which it split from top to bottom, then leaving the mast at level of the deck, it ran along the length of the vessel, killing three men in its course. The second fell two hours later, and running from stem to stern, killed two more men on the deck. The third followed soon after the pilot, sub-pilot, and I being together near the main mast, and the cook coming to ask the pilot if he wished him to serve the supper, the thunderbolt made a small hole in the cook's stomach and burnt off all his hair as one scalds a pig, without doing him any other injury. But, it is true that when this small hole was anointed with coconut oil he cried aloud and experienced acute agony."

The account goes on to say,

"It is curious to read how often in the early days ships were struck by lightening, and to note how little investigations was bestowed upon the subject by the servants of the period."

This lightning incident was not all that uncommon. Often people were killed or injured during thunderstorms. Sometimes, the ship caught fire. If the lightning somehow found its way to the gunpowder room, an explosion often resulted. In later years, a copper rod was placed on the mast running along its entire length, across the deck of the ship and into the water. This prevented further ship losses and deaths from lightning.

Human Error

Human error and carelessness has also taken its toll on ships. One of the great fears on board sailing ships was the possibility of fire while at sea. On the EIC ships, in order to guard against this, no fire was allowed to be kept below decks after eight o'clock at night except for providing warmth for the sick, and then only in lighting the stove. Candles had to be extinguished between decks by nine o'clock and in the cabins by ten o'clock at the latest.

There have been several incidents where the ship's cook accidentally set the ship on fire. In one instance, a drunken cook dug a hole through the brick back of the furnace, giving the fire passage to the ship's side and consequently setting the ship on fire. Fortunately, the fire was contained in time before getting out of control. This cook was afterwards so severely punished by the ship's commander that he did not survive long, dying the following day. In 1824, a careless seaman set fire to a cask of brandy on the *FAME*, an EIC ship that was carrying Sir Stamford Raffles and his wife from Bencoolen in Sumatra to London. Within minutes, the entire ship was ablaze and passengers had to abandon ship. Eventually, the gunpowder on board caught fire and blew up the whole ship.

The gunpowder room was by far the most sensitive area on board seagoing vessels. You're probably wondering how sailors managed to see anything in the dark of the gunpowder room? You're not alone because I have often wondered that myself. What the early sailors did was to cut a hole in the deck and mount a glass crystal in it. During the day, the sun

The *FAME* ablaze off the coast of Sumatra.

THE VUNG TAO CARGO

In 1989, a Vietnamese fisherman snagged his nets on something while out trolling for shellfish a few miles off Con Dao island which lies approximately 100 miles south of Vung Tau on the southern coast of Vietnam. The history of this island is well known – for centuries, it has been a freshwater refueling stop for passing vessels. Unknown to the annoyed fisherman at the time, he had accidentally snagged on a sunken Chinese junk that was laden with fine 17th century Chinese blue and white ceramics. When he retrieved his net, he saw to his amazement that some pieces of porcelain were caught in it.

The fisherman's discovery gradually came to public attention. The junk lay in just 120 feet of water, making it easily accessible to salvagers. It was decided to raise the cargo as a commercial operation with part of the proceeds going towards a Vietnamese museum. The expertise of a Singapore-based Swedish salvager, Sverker Hallstrom, was called upon to conduct the salvage operation.

Judging from the coins and ceramics that were salvaged from the site, the junk had apparently sunk sometime in the late 1600s. The cause of sinking was thought to have been due to fire. This conclusion was obtained from the divers who examined the ship's wooden hull – this was found to be black and charred and appeared to have been burned to the waterline. Perhaps an unlucky cook was to blame for this unfortunate accident!

It was also assumed that the junk was most probably on a voyage from China to the Dutch port of Batavia (now Jakarta in western Java). The "Batavia Roads" was a major trading point and gathering place during the 17th and 18th centuries where oriental ceramics were bartered and in high demand for the growing European market.

After three seasons of diving and recording the site by grid drawings of the hull, the systematic recovery of the junk's cargo was finally completed. The fine Chinese porcelain was auctioned in 1992 by Christie's of Amsterdam and fetched over US$7 million. (The picture above (courtesy of Christie's Images) shows some of the blue and white Ming dynasty porcelain, circa 1690, recovered from the *VUNG TAU* wreck.)

would shine through this crystal, magnifying the light below. In effect, the crystal acted like modern light bulbs. It was the safest way to light the gunpowder room since you definitely wouldn't want to go down there and strike a match! But judging from the number of ships that have been blown up due to carelessness, this could be exactly what some seamen did over the years.

If and when a fire did occur on board a ship and looked like it could possibly get out of hand, the first item to be thrown overboard was the gunpowder. Not surprisingly, it was important to get it overboard as fast as possible. However, when the fire has been successfully put out, the crew would be left with very little on no gunpowder on board, and would then be sailing totally defenceless in a hostile and often ruthless environment – pirates, enemy warships and other dangers could be lurking just around the next island or point.

Unseaworthiness or Timber Dry Rot

One reason for leaks in ships was due to the ship's timbers separating, therefore allowing water to come in. During hot weather, the timbers of the ship that were above water and always dry often began to separate. The only way of preventing this was to keep them wet by constantly throwing seawater on them. Jean Baptist Tavernier, author of *Travels in India* (written in 1676), describes this problem during a voyage in 1652 on large vessel belonging to the king of Golconda:

> *"On the day after and those which followed, the wind became more furious and the sea more disturbed so that when we arrived at the 16th degree, which is the latitude of Goa, the rain, thunder and lightning increased the hurricane, and we were unable to carry any sail except the Simiani, and that half furled, and thus we drove before the wind for many days. We passed the Maldive Islands without being able to see them and our vessel made much water. For it had remained nearly five months in the roads at Gombroon during hot season, for if care is not then taken to wet the timbers which are exposed above water, they open; this is the reason why vessels make so much water when laden. The Dutch do not fail to throw water over theirs both morning and evening, because, without this precaution, one runs the risk of being lost in a tempest!"*

He then goes on to tell of how their pump was not working at the time and that their ship was in much danger of sinking. They afterwards managed to sew together some cow hides which, with the help of the crew and passengers, they were able to use as buckets and scoop out the water. This in effect saved their vessel from sinking.

Even the hull timbers that were wet were susceptible to separate and leak if exposed to prolonged rough weather. This is exactly what happened to the East Indiaman *ELIZABETH* in 1834 as the extract below shows:

> *"3 a.m.   Hard squalls attended with most tremendous gales. In fore and*
> *mizen topsails, reef'd fore sail and close reefed main topsail.*
> *5 a.m.   Heavy sea running, ship laboring much. Hove to under closed*
> *reefed ... topsail, reefed foresail staysail and fore-topmast stay-*
> *sail. Housed fore and mizzen topgallantmasts.*
> *Noon.   Hard gales and a tremendous sea running. Ship laboring much."*

Two days later, there was this entry:

> *"During the late severe gale I find from the heavy laboring of the ship*
> *many seams in the upper and lower decks much opened and the caulking*
> *worked out, and from the great quantity of water ship'd over all and the*
> *ship requiring constant pumping during the above period, I apprehend*
> *considerable damage is done to the cargo."*

Fortunately, all their laboring was not in vain because they got safely across the Indian Ocean and on to China. They were lucky but many others were not so. For every ship wrecked in the open ocean whose location is at least approximately known, there are dozens of others that vanished without a trace. In the earlier days when there was no such thing as telegraphic communication, any vessel that went down with all hands was very unlikely to be located.

How Much Was Lost?

The number of ships that have been lost and wrecked throughout the centuries in Southeast Asian waters is so numerous that it cannot even be guessed at. These waters are an underwater archaeologist's and treasure hunter's dream come true – a vast amount of treasure lies on the seabed virtually untouched.

- The Chinese junks have been braving the Asian waters for centuries and an unestimated amount of these vessels sank over the years, carrying what would be considered today as *priceless* cargo.
- The voyage from Portugal down through the South Atlantic, across the Indian Ocean and into Southeast Asia was long and dangerous. From 1499 through to 1650, some 800 Portuguese vessels sailed from Lisbon of which nearly 150 were never heard of again. Most simply vanished without a trace.
- Of the fabled Manilla galleons which journeyed from Manilla across the Pacific in the quest for Peruvian silver between 1565 through to 1815, 129 galleons were lost, 99 of them in the Philippines alone. The dreaded San Barnardino Straits located between the islands of Luzon and Samar claimed more than its share of ships.
- Between 1600 and 1800, the English East India Company lost over 200 vessels, many of which went to the bottom carrying rich treas-

ures. Some years were particularly unfortunate: in 1808 and 1809, the EIC lost 10 homeward-bound vessels and with them vanished over one million in sterling.

- The Dutch VOC also had its share of misfortune, losing 105 outward-bound ships between 1602 and 1794; homeward-bound losses were even higher with 141 ships lost between 1602 and 1795. A particularly bad period was between the years 1725 to 1749 when the VOC lost 44 homeward-bound vessels.

The value of cargo carried by these vessels was enormous. It is not an exaggeration to say that there is an "El Dorado" in the waters of Southeast Asia. According to *The Treasure Diver's Guide*, by John Potter Jr.:

> *"The Manilla galleons, crossing the Pacific back and forth between Acapulco and the Philippines, 1570–1815. Over US$1.5 million was transported aboard these big ships; at least US$50 million was sunk; US$30 million has never been recovered ...*
>
> *... The 'Spice Route' transverse by the Portuguese and the Dutch carracks and British East Indiamen, joining Europe and the Middle and Far East, 1511–1870. About US$2 million moved across the Indian Ocean (and Southeast Asia); at least US$50 million was lost; scarcely any has been salvaged."*

What Cargo Perished?

Not all the transported cargoes of lost ships in Southeast Asia are of any value today. Having been submerged under the sea for so many years, many would have already perished. The following are some of the perishable items that would be worthless to today's modern salvor:

1. Fine Nanking silk and silk goods from China
2. Tea from China
3. Opium from Bengal (Bangladesh), Damuan (India) and Turkey
4. Cotton from America and China
5. Spices from the Moluccas islands in Indonesia
6. Metals from Europe such as iron
7. Animal skins from America and the British Isles

Non-Perishable Cargo

Many ships also carried valuable cargoes of gold, silver, diamonds, rubies, pearls, precious gems and Chinese and Japanese porcelain and ceramics. Most of these items have been found in ships wrecked in the Southeast Asia region. The value of gold, silver, precious stones, pearls and Asian ceramics lost under the seas is so vast that it is almost beyond estimation.

Gold

Gold, the mysterious soft yellow metal that, even though not many of us know much about it, everyone seems to want it. But most of us may never have the chance to actually recover gold in our lifetime.

For many years, gold was mined out of many Asian countries and shipped back to Europe. Chinese, Indonesian, and Japanese gold was in great demand due to its pureness. Silver, which was scarce in Southeast Asia, was commonly traded for gold. Gold was also brought to the Philippines via the Manilla galleons from the New World. Most of it then ended up being traded among other Asian countries. Some was lost along the route.

The Treasure Diver's Guide states that "The Australian gold shipments, from Melbourne to England via the Straits of Magellan, 1852–1900. Over US$500 million was shipped; several million were lost and never recovered." The total quantity gold shipped from Victoria, Australia from January 1 to February 12, 1853 was 14 tons, 5 cwt. 3 qrs. 14 pounds and 7 ounces. This was only the amount that was shipped in just over one month! In those days, gold was only selling for a mere £3 per ounce.

In the United States, when gold was discovered in California starting the California Gold Rush in 1849, a flood of Chinese coolie immigrants came to the west coast of America in search of their pot of gold. After many years of hard laboring, many of the coolies either sent home much of their findings or they themselves returned to China quite wealthy with gold.

The discovery of alluvial gold in Australia came at about the time of the great California Strike of 1849. That strike upset the theories of geologists and set every man on the world's frontiers searching for the elusive metal. When gold was discovered in Australia in 1851, Chinese coolies also flooded there in search of their rainbow. Between 1852 and 1857 when the rush to the diggings was at its height, 100,000 Englishmen, 60,000 Irish, 50,000 Scottish, 8,000 Germans, 4,000 Welsh, 3,000 Americans, 1,500 French and no less than 25,000 Chinese coolies landed on Australian shores. In 1862, several ships were hurried across with diggers from Melbourne to Port Chalmers for a second Australian gold rush to Gabriel's Gully.

It was not only coolies but also Europeans and Americans on board the homeward ships that carried gold. Most passengers paid good money for the privilege of getting seasick during their journey on board these vessels. To give you an example of the fee that each passenger paid for his passage, the ship *EAGLE*, which left Melbourne on September 2, 1852 bound for England, charged each passenger £50 to £60 sterling for the voyage to England. This gives some idea of how much money there was in the captain's safe in addition to the gold shipment on board. Depending on their size, some ships could carry anywhere from 500 to 800 or more passengers per trip. The *EAGLE* also had a gold shipment of 150,000 ounces. Fortunately for her, she sailed safely across the Indian Ocean.

JEWELLED CARGO

It was common for ships to carry a large payroll in order to pay for personnel, goods, supplies and food during their long voyage at sea. Money and jewellery of officers and passengers alone sometimes added up to more than the ship's registered bullion value.

As far as paying customs and excise taxes is concerned, not much has changed between 1600 and today. Many people hid and smuggled gold, silver and precious stones to avoid paying taxes. One legal way to get out of it was seen in the practice that "if you could wear it, it was classified as personal jewellery and was therefore untaxable". So the old trick was to struggle up the gangway on board the vessel loaded down with jewellery, wearing long, elaborate gold chains on the neck, thick gold bracelets on each wrist and gold rings studded with precious stones on each finger. It is highly likely that some of the long gold chains recovered from shipwrecks could once have belonged to some unfortunate tax-evading passenger!

Silver

Silver was the main medium of exchange in Asia. For many years, Asian traders preferred Spanish American *reals* because of their high silver content over European silver. Portuguese, Dutch, and English traders bought their silver in Europe or the Philippines at a cheaper rate and used it to purchase goods in Asia where it had a higher rate of exchange. Towards the end of the 16th century, the annual drain of silver from Mexico was in upwards of 7 million *pesos* (or pieces of eight *reals*). By 1651–1660, this had dwindled down to a little over a million *pesos* per year. The silver from Central and South America shipped across the Pacific by the Manilla galleons through the Philippines to China, India, and Japan amounted to around 5 million *pesos* per year on average. During this time, the Spaniards preferred to use the Pacific route as it was relatively safe from attack by the English and Dutch who had fleets in the Atlantic and Caribbean.

In the early 1600s, Dutch vessels carried such coinage as Netherlands large silver coins (*rijksdaalders)* and German *thalers*, weighing between 25 and 28 grams. These German *thalers* were equivalent to the English crown or five shilling piece containing roughly 26 grams of pure silver. In fact, the abovementioned coins were found on the Dutch East Indiamen BATAVIA which was wrecked in the Abrolhos Islands on the west coast of Australia on June 4, 1629. At the time, this ship was bound for Batavia.

VOC silver bars and coins recovered from the BREDENHOF which sank on a reef near the Cape of Good Hope, South Africa (courtesy of Christie's Images).

By the mid-1600s, Spanish pieces of eight *reals* were also commonly carried on Dutch vessels. These were of the rough COB type from Mexico under Spain (COB is short for *Cabo de Barra* meaning "end of the bar" in Spanish). This was a rough method of minting by hammering out a thin bar of silver which was heated and struck on the end between obverse and reverse dies; the resulting coin was then chiselled off and trimmed roughly to weight with shears. One *marc* (approximately 8 ounces of troy) of silver had to produce 67 *reals* of coinage, but the final gross tally was by weight rather than count. Most coinage was struck in the form of eight *real* pieces with a smaller number of four and two *real* pieces. The vast silver resources of Spanish America allowed Spain to dominate the commercial world and flood the market with Spanish money, thus becoming an international means of exchange. This persisted as such until the first quarter of the 19th century when Spain lost her colonies and her dominant role in world commerce.

Money Chests

Coinage or bullion (often called specie) was loaded and carried in money chests. These chests varied in shape and size, depending on the year in question and the country of origin. The number of coins in a chest could range from as little as 1,000 to as much as 10,000 or more. Money chests were very strongly built – they had to be due to the amount of weight they were required to carry. Some of the wooden chests were even lined inside with a copper sheathing for extra strength and protection. Later chests were even made of iron. All had a lock of some sort for obvious reasons.

It was the practice of the Dutch VOC up to the year 1629 to pack 8,000 large silver coins per chest (as found on the BATAVIA). A chest such as this would weigh upwards of 240 kilograms and would have required several men to handle. After 1629, the number of *rijksdaalders* per chest was reduced to 4,000 for easier handling (about 120 kilograms per chest).

In 1885, nine chests out of 10 chests lost were recovered by divers off the Spanish mail steamer ALFONSO XII sunk off Point Gando in the Grand Canary Island. Each chest contained 10,000 gold coins, bringing the total to 90,000 coins recovered. The total monetary value of the 10 chests was $500,000. The divers therefore recovered a total of $450,000 in gold. That would mean that each gold coin was worth $5,000 dollars. Unfortunately, during the six month salvage operation, two divers lost their lives.

According to *Diving for the Griffin* by Charles Daggett and Christopher Shaffer, when referring to the amount of specie carried by EIC ships in the year 1748, "each of these [chests] contained the standard weight of specie, 290 pounds 8 ounces, or 2,648 ounces".

In the book, *The Chronicles of the East India Company's Trading to China, 1635–1834* by Hosea Ballow Morse, " ... during the season 1792 the Company had 16 ships of 12,271 tons at Canton. The ships brought silver in 180 chests (= 627,840 oz. = 720,000 dollars = tls. 518,400)." To estimate how many coins were in each chest, I simply divided 720,000 (total amount of coins) by 180 (total amount of chests) and came to the figure of about 4,000 coins per chest. Then, according to the same book, in 1803, the amount of coins per chest had dropped to approximately 3,500. In 1805, the figure dropped even more to about 1,000 coins per chest.

Whether this EIC figure of 1,000 coins per chest increased or decreased after the year 1805, I cannot say because there were no further listings of coins or chests in the above book. The pattern seems to be that the chests were getting smaller in size, probably for easier handling. I was interested in the amount of coins per chest (on English ships) because sometimes accounts of shipwrecks only tell you that a vessel was lost with a certain number of chests of treasure on board. Therefore, if you know the approximate amount of coins in each chest during a particular year, at least you would have some idea of the amount of treasure you are dealing with.

For instance, I had this problem with the EIC ship *VANSITTART*. The initial account said that 10 chests of gold and silver coins were lost with this ship. Not having any idea as to the amount of coins each chest would have contained, I was stumped. Even a well-known British researcher who specializes in English East Indiamen could not answer the question as to the number of coins per chest. I am still searching for an answer.

Oriental Ceramics

The ceramic and stoneware trade history of north and Southeast Asia began as far back as the first or second century A.D. By the 7th century Tang dynasty, trading in ceramics had become a big business. The wares of northern China were shipped to as far away as Persia (modern day Iran) overland via the Silk Road. By the end of the Tang dynasty, southern wares were being shipped by sea to Asian countries. Shortly afterwards, the Middle East and North Africa were trading these ceramics as well.

Chinese porcelain and stoneware reached Southeast Asia as early as the 9th century. From southern China, the junks took one of two routes: one route was down the west coast of the Philippines past Borneo and Sulawesi to the Moluccas islands; the other route followed the coastline of Vietnam, Thailand and the Malay peninsula. From there, they either turned south to Java or Sumatra or headed west out to the Indian Ocean.

On the Southeast Asian porcelain trade, C.R. Boxer in *The Dutch Seaborne Empire, 1600–1800* states that:

> "The substantial home demand was surpassed by the greater amount that was re-exported to other countries, so that the shipments from the Far East to the northern Netherlands increased rapidly. More than three million pieces of Chinese porcelain were shipped to Europe in Dutch East Indiamen between 1602 and 1657, followed by about 190,000 pieces of Japanese porcelain between 1659 and 1682, when China was disturbed by civil strife. Apart from exports to Europe, several millions of pieces (mainly

Chinese) were transhipped at Batavia for disposal in the markets of Indonesia, Malaya, India, and Persia, etc."

He goes on to say,

"During the 18th century the polychrome, monochrome and enamelled wares steadily gained favour in most European markets, though blue and white still continued to set the tone in the Dutch Republic itself."

Japanese porcelain was commonly traded with the Dutch between the years 1683 till 1757. Trade was officially renewed again in the year 1820.

American ships also transported Chinese porcelain to the United States and Europe from the late 1700s onwards. At that time, Canton was a major port in China where European and US vessels traded in oriental goods. In 1784, the first American ship to call at port that year was the EMPRESS OF THE SEA from New York. For her outward voyage back, she took on tea, nankeen (cotton silk), Chinaware, wolves silk and cassia. The amount of Chinaware was valued at a cost of $2,500 Spanish dollars (this was measured as 962 *picals* where one *pical* is equivalent to 133 and-one-third pounds in weight). From the figures given, it is obvious that 962 *picals* of Chinaware is quite a large amount. The total amount of Chinaware exported from Canton during 1784 was 4,465 *picals*, via English, Dutch, Danish, French and American ships.

By 1818, no less than 44 vessels registered under the US flag called at Canton, importing $7.3 million in silver specie. The exports to the US during the same year were reported at $9 million. Between

A ceramic plate recovered from the GLASS WRECK (see Chapter 4 – Search for the Lost Treasures of Malacca).

1805 to 1833, US ships imported a total specie value of $88,819,597 into Canton. In 1827, the Americans joined England in the practice of taking bills on London from the United States to Canton (instead of specie) and selling them there to the traders wishing to make remittances to India. In 1833, this practice was developed fully by US ships trading at Canton.

A Fortune in Treasure

Southeast Asian waters are an underwater archaeologist's and treasure-hunter's dream come true with vast amounts of treasure lying on the sea bed virtually untouched. The value of these lost goods may run into billions of dollars. In fact, the estimated value of one ship alone, the Portuguese prizeship *FLOR DO MAR* which was wrecked off the northeastern coast of Sumatra in 1511 ranges from US$1 billion upwards.

Many Southeast Asian countries today are realizing the value of the priceless items that lie on their seabed, not just in monetary terms but also in historical terms. Many countries are opening up their waters to salvage operations, welcoming foreign salvage companies who are willing to invest in operations there. And why shouldn't they? After all, the countries have nothing to lose and everything to gain: the foreign salvage company funds the operations 100% while the country issues the survey and salvage license, provides any protection needed and, in turn, receives an agreed percentage of the items sold. With any luck, all parties will be one day be arranging for the auction of the goods recovered.

3
RESEARCHING WRECKS

Having been two years involved with the search for the Portuguese East Indiaman FLOR DO MAR, I became personally involved with researching shipwrecks. Let me tell you that once I started, I could not stop. I loved the research and everything about it. Some people may think that it is boring but I feel a certain excitement in uncovering, deciphering and putting together clues from various different sources to determine the most probable final resting position of a lost vessel.

If you are planning a serious attempt to go out and locate a sunken ship for whatever reasons, you need to have properly researched your potential target thoroughly. In this way, your expenses, search and recovery time will be minimized. Research plays such a vital role in a successful search and salvage operation that its importance cannot be stressed enough here. Without it, no one should even so much as *think* of going after a sunken vessel.

The lack of funds, insufficient research or inexperienced personnel spells failure for any potential salvage operation. Unless you have a bottomless pocket and plenty of time on your hands, there are certain questions that you need answered.

What to Ask When Researching Wrecks

Here is an example of only a few of those questions you'll need answers for *before* you even begin your actual search if you are serious about your project. At first glance, some of these questions may seem painfully silly but let me explain further.

1. **Did the ship in question really even exist?**
    Over the years, countless books have been written about shipwrecks and lost treasures. Believe me, that is exactly what many of these books are – *tales* or vividly made up stories by some bored writer on a Sunday afternoon. It's funny but many of these tales of "treasure chests being guarded by a large octopus surrounded by sharks on a sunken ship with a skeleton at the wheel" that have been passed around over years tend to make people believe in them without question. Check the records and prove beyond a shadow of a doubt the your ship was not just a ghost ship.

2. **Did the ship actually sink?**
    Lots of ships have *hit* on a hidden reef or shoal and later managed

to get off undamaged. On May 1, 1788, the American ship WARREN HASTINGS on her return voyage from China to America was grounded in the Gaspar Straits, Indonesia. A very well-known researcher actually told me that the WARREN HASTINGS had sunk there. After much time and research, I found this to be incorrect; according to the records, the ship later got off the shoal undamaged and continued on its homeward voyage. It just goes to show that sometimes you don't know whose word to accept. Sometimes, the accounts get confusing or the story gets distorted, and the next thing you know, someone comes up with a statement that the ship sank.

3. **Where exactly did it sink?**
   Precise latitude and longitude readings are almost never given because sailors will not have had the time to take these on board the chaos of a sinking ship. Some accounts may tell of a ship sinking 30 miles off the coast or provide some vague reference point. Descriptions by survivors such as being close to spitting distance of the shore can also be notoriously exaggerated or inaccurate in the feverish rush to abandon ship. Even if a precise location is mentioned, remember that this may not reflect the ship's final resting position as currents and tides may have moved the ship over the years.

4. **What were the weather conditions at the time?**
   Suppose the ship hit on the north side of a reef during a storm but did not sink immediately. Well, if the storm happened to be blowing towards the east, the ship's final resting place would appear to be towards the east too. Unfortunately, it is not as simple as that. Remember to take into account the direction of the sea's currents. In this way, you would be able to drastically cut down your search area and time. After studying all the factors involved at the time of the sinking, you should be able to come up with a logical estimation as to the final resting place of the vessel. If you know the exact date and approximate time of sinking, a meteorologist can accurately calculate tide and current direction at that time.

5. **What cargo was lost with the ship and was any of it recovered at that time?**
   This is very important and will determine whether or not a salvage operation is even worth investing in. Check the ship's manifest to see what cargo it was carrying. Reports of the wreck may also tell you if any cargo was saved at the time of wrecking.

6. **Were there any salvage attempts at a later date and, if so, what was recovered?**
   Imagine spending thousands of dollars, not even mentioning the

amount of time wasted, only to find that your ship was salvaged at a later date after your investment! That would be enough bad news to ruin anyone's day. Do check whether any previous salvage operations have been made.

Perhaps you can see now that those questions were not so silly after all. The bottom line is this – if you're serious about salvaging a wreck, these questions and more like them must be answered. The only way it can be done effectively is through proper research.

Even though you may have located a shipwreck, remember that without research, without a story, you have nothing. Research is the key to success if you plan to have any kind of auction of the items recovered. Research provides the information that pulls in the crowd at auctions, it is what makes people *feel* the history, the story, the tragedy of it all.

Treasure Hunting Around Reefs

Reefs or shoals that are located along the major shipping routes are especially interesting hunting grounds for treasure salvors as they sometimes are a rich repository of wrecks.

If you have plenty of time and the funds in your hands, one search technique is to go to a known dangerous reef or shoal that is located in the track of shipping routes and simply start surveying in the deeper water around it. This technique was used by Michael Hatcher when he chanced upon the GELDERMALSEN. A small boat towing a side scan sonar and proton magnetometer (see Chapter 4 for an explanation of these instruments) simultaneously would be all that is required for the initial survey. You may find not just one but *several* interesting targets during this search. Once you have dived on them and proved that there is something there, you can then research that particular area and try to find out what ships have wrecked on or near it.

Looking at any of the maritime charts today, you may notice that many reefs and shoals are named after ships and even named after ship captains. Did you ever wonder how those names came about? The most common reasons why a reef or shoal is named after a ship or captain are as follows:

Lighthouse at Cape Rachado 57 kilometers north of Malacca. In 1606, Portuguese and Dutch naval fleets battled here for control of Malacca.

The ship wrecked on that reef or shoal

This is an either/or situation – either the ship hit the reef and wrecked on it, or it hit the reef, floated off and then sank *nearby*.

For instance, the *BAMBEEK*, a Dutch East Indiamen of 845 tons under the command of Captain Evert Doedes, was on a voyage from China bound for the Netherlands when on January 1, 1702, the ship got stranded and was wrecked on a shoal off the Malacca coast (Cape Rachado). This uncharted shoal is now known as Bambek Shoal on modern charts. However, just because a reef or shoal is named after a ship that was lost there does not necessarily mean that the ship also sank right there. In 1789, the EIC ship *VANSITTART* hit on a hidden shoal while surveying the Gaspar Straits in Indonesia. The vessel immediately started taking on water but did not sink on the spot. To save the vessel and treasure on board, Captain Lestock Wilson headed the doomed ship to the nearest island, only just managing to reach it before the ship grounded. Today, the shoal that the vessel struck on is known as Vansittart's Shoal. This is one example of a reef or shoal named after a vessel that hit it, floated off and then sank elsewhere.

Ideally, the ships that hit on a reef, floated off and sank in deeper water somewhere in the vicinity are the preferable targets for salvors; they tend to be more interesting because of the fact that they sank virtually intact and in deeper waters, which made salvage attempts in earlier days difficult or impossible. Sometimes the ships sank in an unknown location which was far from the reef that it hit, which also hinders the salvagers in locating the vessel. Because these ships did not break up on the reef, their

THE HATCHER JUNK

In June 1983, Captain Michael Hatcher, an Australian who was already a highly successful tin ingot salvage diver, located and recovered a cargo of some 25,000 pieces of 17th century oriental ceramics from an unknown wrecked Chinese junk in the South China Sea. Upon closer examination of the cargo, archaeologists estimated that the vessel must have sunk no earlier than the spring of 1643. This conclusion was made only after carefully dating the latest or most newly made porcelain recovered from the wreck. This also assumed that the vessel had sailed shortly after the loading of this newly made cargo and had sunk soon afterwards.

A total of 22,178 pieces of mostly Jingdezhen blue and white porcelain (there were also groups of celadon, blanc-de-chine, colored wares and provincial blue and white) were auctioned in 1983 for an unknown amount by Christie's of Amsterdam.

In 1985, Captain Hatcher returned to the China junk wreck site and recovered another 2,000 pieces or porcelain. These were later auctioned through a London dealer, Heirloom and Howard, for an undisclosed amount.

cargo is more likely to be still be intact and unbroken. This was the case with the VOC ship GELDERMALSEN which was wrecked in January 1751 while on her homeward voyage from China. The ship hit on an uncharted reef in the Riau archipelago (Indonesia), floated off into deeper waters and sank. When it was salvaged by Captain Michael Hatcher in 1985, the cargo of fine Ming and Ching dynasty porcelain was found to be virtually undamaged.

On April 7, 1845, the COLUMBIAN, bound from Sydney to Singapore, also ran onto a hidden shoal in the Gaspar Straits without getting stuck. The captain anchored at once but the crew were obliged to abandon the ship in a sinking state the following day. These are just two examples of ships that hit on a reef or shoal, floated off and sank intact in deeper waters.

The ship hit upon, and/or got stuck on a reef or shoal, afterwards getting off with little or no damage

Many reefs and shoals were named in this way too. Although they did not sink there, sometimes the ships were stranded there for hours or even days before getting off. In such desperate situations, the captain would do anything in his power to lighten and save the ship. This includes throwing overboard cannons, anchors, cargo and ballast.

On May 23, 1802, the American ship, SEVERN, bound from China to New York, struck on a coral shoal. After throwing overboard 30 tons of ballast, it got off during the next high tide. On today's charts, this danger spot is now known as Severn Shoal located in the Gaspar Straits, Indonesia.

The ship discovered that reef or shoal

In this case, the ship did not hit or wreck on it or even touch it. It may have passed nearby and noticed an uncharted reef. The normal routine was then to anchor nearby and take latitude and longitude readings and report its position upon reaching the next civilized port. The reef's position was then added to the latest nautical charts so that the other passing ships would know of this danger in the future. It is not hard to imagine that this "charting of undiscovered reefs" was a long, slow, drawn-out process that took many years of trial and error to accomplish. Over the years, just how many ships were lost is anybody's guess.

In short, research is the only way that you will be able to get the answers and know the real truth about the ship's story. Not only will you learn more about Asian maritime history, but you will most probably find out that most of the ship's stories are quite fascinating and hardly ever boring.

THE GELDERMALSEN'S FABULOUS NANKING CARGO

On November 30, 1751, the 1150-ton Dutch East Indiaman *GELDERMALSEN* departed from Canton, China for a homeward-bound voyage back to the Netherlands via the Cape of Good Hope. The ship's cargo at the time was valued at 714,936 Dutch *florins*. It had on board, among other things, over 140,000 pieces of fine Ming dynasty blue and white porcelain (which was packed in the tea crates) and 149 Chinese shoe-shaped gold ingots.

All went well on the voyage until the night of January 3, 1752 when, what most feel was due to a result of navigational error, screams were suddenly heard from the boatswain on watch. He saw breakers, always the sign of a reef near the surface, and yelled for the steersman to swing the ship off its southerly course. But it was too late and the vessel hit heavily on the reef. After an emergency order to reset the sails was given by Captain Morel, the ship tore free of the reef and headed in an easterly direction. At this point, there was much chaos and confusion among the crew which must have affected Captain Morel's judgement. He then gave new instructions for re-setting the sails which unavoidably slewed the ship back onto a southerly track. This time, the ship suffered major damage upon slamming into the reef a second time. The ship later freed itself of the reef, floated off and then sank in deeper water.

Of the 112 persons on board, only 32 survived, arriving back at Batavia in two boats a week later. Among those lost were Captain Morel, the first and second mate, 30 or more soldiers, the rest being passengers and other crew members. Also lost with them was the *GELDERMALSEN's* treasure which was later to be referred to as "The Nanking Cargo".

Having studied maritime history for some time, Michael Hatcher knew that if there was a dangerous reef in a major shipping route, there had to have been some unfortunate ships lost on that reef over the years. He therefore decided to single out and survey on and around one such reef located in Indonesia's Riau Archipelago. Little did he know at the time that the particular reef that he had chosen was in fact the very same reef on which the ill-fated VOC ship *GELDERMALSEN* had wrecked on over two centuries ago.

After weeks of surveying on and around this reef, Hatcher and his partner Max Rahm chanced upon the sunken *GELDERMALSEN*, a find that undoubted changed their lives and those of many others. During the 1985 salvage operation, over 140,000 pieces of fabulous Ming dynasty porcelain and 125 Chinese shoe-shaped gold ingots were recovered from the sunken vessel. The Nanking Cargo was later auctioned by Christie's of Amsterdam for a staggering US$15 million.

Research Sources

You can research for shipwrecks in most major libraries. I did quite a lot of research in Singapore at the National Library (located at Stamford Road) which has a special reference section totally dedicated to materials on Southeast Asian history. There are several thousand books in the SEAS room, many of which are very old, so are available for viewing only on microfilm. If you wish to use the SEAS room, permission must be requested from the library. A company letter is advisable. Other libraries in Singapore that have information on shipwrecks are the National University library and the Institute of Southeast Asian Studies' library.

This section discusses research sources available in Singapore. Other libraries and museums in Southeast Asia should also be consulted; for instance, the Maritime Museum in Malacca, the National Library in Kuala Lumpur, Malaysia and the national libraries in Calcutta or Bombay, India which would have records of EIC and British merchant vessels. Libraries in Manila and Jakarta would also have records of Spanish and Dutch wrecks though these will not be in English.

Newspapers

Once you have found the name of the vessel you wish to pursue and the year of sinking, there are two ways of proceeding with research.

1. **If the vessel sank after 1827**

   This was the first year that the *Singapore Chronicle and Commercial Register* was published, and there is a good chance that you may be able to find information on this on microfilm records at the Singapore National Library. Most of the ships that sank after 1827 would be listed in the newspapers. However, if you do not know the date of wrecking, this could lead to a long drawn out process of searching through hundreds of rolls of microfilm. It is best to know the date or at least the year.

   Three early Straits Settlements newspapers were the *Singapore Chronicle and Commercial Register* (January 1827 to September 1837), the *Singapore Free Press and Mercantile Advertiser* (October 1835 to December 1866) and the *Pinang Gazette and Straits Chronicle* (April 1838 to December 1893). There are also numerous other newspapers in various languages.

   As there were a considerable number of Europeans and Americans residing in Asia, most Asian

> —ooo—
> **LOSS OF THE *EMMA*.**
> The American ship *Emma* Capt. Sherman from Macao bound to Singapore was totally lost on the Paracels on the 13th February at 4.30 a.m. two days after leaving Macao.
> We are sorry to state that this shipwreck has been attended by a great loss of life.
> The vessel struck aft first at low water and immediately broke in half. Several attempts were made to get ropes fast to the rocks, the boats were lowered and quickly capsized and broken up.
> Captain Sherman and two of his crew, were last seen drifting out to sea, and no hope can scarcely now be entertained of their safety.
> Many of the men refused to leave the wreck, and were killed or drowned when the bowsprit and fore part of the ship fell in.

The Singapore Free Press (May 8, 1862) reports the loss of a ship in the Paracel Islands in the South China Sea.

countries had some kind of English language newspapers from the early to mid-1800s, and in some places, even earlier. For instance, Americans were residing in Canton since the year 1714 and the English and other Europeans were there many years before that. Most of these newspapers reported some shipping news throughout the years. In China, at least five well known English language newspapers that were published were the *Canton Press, China Mail, Friend of China, North China Herald*, and *Daily Press*. In Hong Kong there was a paper called the *Hongkong Register*, and in Bengal (India), the *Bengal Harkart*. Also from India were *Friend of India, Bombay Gazette, Calcutta Englishman* and *Bombay Times*. If you can read Dutch, the *Batavia Handelsblad* and the *Javasche Courant* was published in Batavia.

2.   **If your vessel sank before 1827**
There is not much detailed information on newspaper microfilm before 1827 in the National Library in Singapore. In this case, you should at least know the ship's nationality (Portuguese, Dutch, English, French or American), so that you can visit or write to information sources in the country in question to investigate further. Some addresses that you can to write for such information are listed at the end of this chapter.

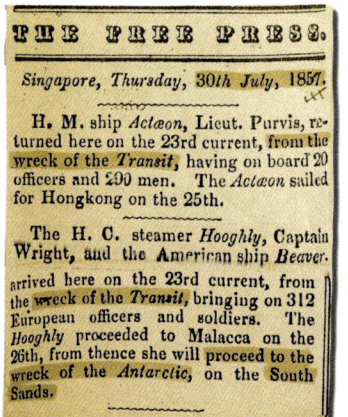

A July 30, 1857 report in the Singapore Free Press carries news of the loss of the TRANSIT and the rescue of its crew and passengers by other ships.

The New York Times, founded in 1851, can be used for ships that sank during and after that year Many other American newspapers are listed in the following two books: *History and Bibliography of American Newspapers, 1690–1820* by Clarence S. Brigham (in two volumes), and *the Dictionary of Newspapers and Periodicals*, by N.W. Ayer and Sons, which covers the period until 1880. However, none of these are available in Singapore.

A newspaper called *Lloyd's List* was founded in London in 1740 and is still published today. It contains information pertaining to British shipping movements, as well as vessels of other nationality. In the early Straits Settlement's newspapers, *Lloyd's* advertised for all shipping companies to report any shipping losses. It also reports any information regarding salvaging of ships. *Lloyd's List* is available in England and the United States but, unfortunately, not in Singapore.

Books
Any old books regarding sailing directions are always an invaluable guide to the researcher. These books were written for the captains of ships on the

safest sailing routes to take and how to avoid the many dangerous hidden reefs and shoals. Often, they will tell you what ships have hit, grounded or sank on which particular reefs and shoals, usually describing them in great detail.

One such book which I have to referred to many times here in Singapore is *The India Directory* written by James Horsburgh and published in 1841 (in two volumes). In it, you will find sailing directions from Africa to South America, thoroughly covering the Northeast and Southeast Asian regions. A book of sailing directions covering the Gaspar Straits area is *Sailing Directions for the Banka Straits*, translated from the Dutch records in 1847 by Lieutenant H.D.A. Smits. This book details most, if not all, of the dangers in the Gaspar Straits area.

A comprehensive list of all of the old books available in the Singapore National Library on Stamford Road can be found on the rare books titles list. Due to their age, most will only be available on microfilm. A comprehensive book that lists shipwrecks throughout the world is *The Treasure Diver's Guide* by John S. Potter Jr.

Using Researchers

If there is no library in your vicinity, as long as you know the name of the ship you are interested in, you can write to any of the addresses (according to the ship's nationality) that I have listed at the end of this chapter. You can also hire someone to research for you, again by writing to the same addresses. However, most good researchers will be quite busy and may sometimes take up to three months or more before they can get any answers back to you. If you are in a hurry, this can be quite frustrating. They normally charge by the hour, plus you have to pay for any additional expenses (such as phone calls, faxes and mailing costs). Their research fees vary: for example, a British researcher may charge £15 per hour, while a Dutch researcher charges 25 Dutch guilders per hour. You will have to send them an international money order in advance, usually in their home currency.

In order to save time, you should tell them *everything* that you know about the ship in question – the ship's name, date and place (general) of sinking, if known. From this information, your researcher will hopefully be able to walk straight up to the book that will have the answers you need. Otherwise, searching through hundreds of books (or microfilm) could take months and cost lots of money.

I hope you understand the importance of research by now. Once you have all of your research in hand, you can now start to seriously think about your search and salvage operations.

SALVAGING WRECKS
– PRESERVATION OR PLUNDER?

Upon learning the ship's background, many of us would probably come to appreciate salvaged cargoes and maybe even to own a small piece of this history ourselves. To some marine archaeologists, this statement may sound unprofessional and selfish, but the fact of the matter is that treasure salvors not only love what they do, they also have a deep respect for the vessel that they are salvaging. I think that I speak for most of them in saying:

"We all are fascinated with maritime history and want to excavate, study and share this fascination with anyone who is willing to join us by way of either purchasing items we have recovered, reading books we have written or watching our documentary films that relate to wrecks and underwater salvage. Our excavation intentions are in no way meant to damage or destroy any part of the vessels we are working on.

Hopefully, during our excavations, we will bring to light new and exciting finds and maritime historical information to share with the world. If at all feasible (meaning we are not hampered by strong currents, bad visibility or bad weather), we will do our best to carefully document and photograph every major find while at the same time keeping within a realistic working time scale."

Referring to the last sentence, you must remember that most of these projects are funded by private investors, and therefore, our working time schedule is often limited. Being myself an avid member of the American Society For Amateur Archaeology (ASAA) and subscriber to *Plus Ultra Newsletter* (which has much information concerning underwater archaeology), I am quite aware of the importance and preservation of maritime history.

Of course, treasure hunters are in it for the money too: it is our job, the line of work that we have chosen. But to be honest, big money is far and few between. For every successful treasure hunt that you hear about on the news, there are a hundred others you will never hear about that ended in failure. The major reasons for this are insufficient research and lack of funds.

Salvaging wrecks is also not as glamorous a job as everyone thinks it is. Sometimes we survey the ocean for months on end, staring at an empty side scan sonar image without so much as finding a single interesting target. We often dive in strong currents, black water and river mud – more mud than you could ever imagine. This is the *real deal*. But I still wouldn't trade it for any other job!

REFERENCE SOURCES

The following is a list of sources from whom you can request information on ships of European and American nationalities:

FRANCE

Archives Nationales
60 rue des Francs-Bourgeois
75141 Paris

Bibliotheque Nationale
58 rue Richelieu
75084 Paris Cedex

Note: I have not written the above two sources and so cannot comment on their response. At worst, they should at least be able to recommend some other places to write to for information on French shipwrecks.

Musee de Marine
Paris 75011

GERMANY

Deutsches Schiffahrtsmuseum
Van-Ronzelen-Str.
2850 Bremerhaven

Militargeschichtliches
Forschungsamt
Freiburg im Breisgau

PORTUGAL

Museu de Marinha
Praca Do Imperio
1400 Lisboa

THE NETHERLANDS

Rijksuniversiteit Leiden
Subfaclteit der Geschiedenis
Post Box 9515, 2300 Leiden
The Netherlands

SPAIN

Archivo General de Simancas
Carretera de Salamanca S/N
47130 SIMANCAS (VALLADOLID)

Archivo Historico National
Ministerio De Cultura
SERRANO, 115
28006 - Madrid

Archives of the Indies
Seville

UNITED KINGDOM

The British Library
Oriental and India Office Collections
197 Blackfriars Road
London SE1 8NG

Note: The British Library will do a limited amount or research free of charge. However, staff are very busy so expect the usual three months waiting period. You will be charged for any photocopies and postage.

UNITED STATES

The Mariners' Museum
100 Museum Drive
Newport News, Virginia 23606-3798

Note : No research fee is charged but the time spent on any patron is very limited. They cannot have a running correspondence that will require extensive research. They can, however, recommend to you a freelance researcher.

National Archives and Records Adminstration
Eight Street and Pennsylvania Avenue
N.W., Washington, D.C. 20408

Note: This library does not charge a research fee. However, the staff are very busy so it may take some months before they can respond. As of November 1993, the National Archives moved to a new building, Archives II, in College Park, Maryland, and to the downtown building in Washington. The move will continue through 1996, during which time, various record groups will be closed for research and reference, including requests for information and reproductions.

4

SEARCH AND SALVAGE

A proper shipwreck salvage requires a team of skilled personnel such as experienced divers and supervisors, photographers, marine archaeologists, specialized hydrographic surveyors and electronic technicians. High-tech equipment (some of which is explained later in this chapter) for surveying and diving is also required. Your chances of success without the aforementioned are slim to none.

This book was not written to try and convince the average weekend recreational scuba diver to go out and attempt to salvage a wreck. Not only is this a very unwise thing to do, you could also land yourself in deep trouble with the government of the country in whose waters you are attempting to salvage a wreck. Without obtaining permission in the form

BEWARE LOOTERS!

With the many exciting and previously out of the way islands and reefs now opening up to scuba divers, it is inevitable that some old shipwrecks will be discovered. Fortunately (from the point of view of preserving wrecks from looters), many of these ships that sank a hundred or more years ago won't be recognized by a diver with an untrained eye. These wrecks could be either covered by sand, mud or marine growth such as coral reefs, and may just look like a pile of rubble.

Of course, anyone seeing the remains of a noticeable shipwreck for the first time will be awed and fascinated, to say the least. Wild dreams of lost treasures, such as silver, gold, diamonds and oriental ceramics are enough to make even the most calm and collected person loose his or her better judgment. Sure, everyone wants to take home a souvenir or two. However, scuba divers should beware! Most Southeast Asian countries today are now aware of their maritime history and realize that their waters hold many a lost vessel laden with rich cargo. And they don't take kindly to the looting and pillaging of these wrecks.

Heavy fines and even jail sentences are becoming a common deterrent by these countries to protect their wrecks. Indonesia, Malaysia and Vietnam are three countries that have already enforced their wreck pillaging laws on foreign and local divers caught red-handed with the recovered items still dripping from their goodie bags. Most were sentenced to jail terms, fines or even both. Let me tell you, sweating in a foreign jail is no way to end a nice dive trip! Pleading ignorance will not convince them of your innocence either: maybe a few years ago this trick could have worked, but not anymore. They're all wise to it now!

of salvage licenses from them, you are considered a looter and may even end up spending some time in the local jail.

Getting Salvage Licenses

All countries have certain regulations requiring prospective salvors to obtain proper licenses before beginning salvage operations in territorial waters.

Prospective salvors planning to investigate or salvage shipwrecks in the territorial waters of Asian countries are strongly advised to contact the proper government authorities and comply with all salvage regulations.

Indonesia

Indonesia officially opened its waters up to shipwreck salvage groups in 1989. The terms (as of February 1994) between the government and salvors are as follows:

1. The government gets 50% of any goods recovered and sold (this is *after* deduction of the project's costs).
2. The license cost is Rupiah 100,000,000. This is refundable at the end of the project. The license duration for sea projects is five years; for land projects, it is two years. (Another US$10,000 to US$15,000 may be necessary to pay other government departments.)

Malaysia

Malaysia officially opened its waters up to shipwreck salvage groups in the early 1980s. The terms (as of February 1994) between the government and salvors are as follows:

1. The government gets 35% of any goods recovered and sold.
2. License guarantee fee for project start up is MR200,000. This is refundable at the end of the project.
3. There is no time limit on the license.

Vietnam

Vietnam has officially opened its waters up to shipwreck salvage groups. With the lifting of the US embargo in February 1994, American companies can now legally do business with Vietnam. The terms (as of February 1994) between the government and salvers are as follows:

1. The government gets a previously agreed percentage of any goods recovered and sold.
2. There is no licence fee.
3. The license duration is two years for sea projects.

Philippines

There have been several salvage groups working in and around the Philippines throughout the years. It is the land of the famous Manilla galleons, the richest ships of their time, which every treasure hunter dreams of salvaging some day.

The Law of the Sea

Determining the law of the sea is a touchy subject in Southeast Asia. Although you may have located a shipwreck several miles out to sea in what you think are international waters, don't take this for granted! In this region, there seems to be little consensus of what constitutes international waters as far as salvaging shipwrecks goes.

Living proof of this was seen in the case of the THAILAND JUNK wreck (see opposite) that was located some 60 miles offshore in the Gulf of Thailand. Not surprisingly, the salvagers here thought themselves to be in international waters but the Thai government felt differently. Not only was the operation ceased, the Royal Thai Navy boarded the salvage vessel and confiscated all the recovered goods.

A 12-mile territorial limit is the commonly accepted limit for most countries throughout the world – that is, no foreign ship can legally enter this zone for fishing or any other commercial activities without permission. However, a country's economic zone can be extended out to as much as 200 miles offshore for natural resources, such as gas and oil. But does a shipwreck fall into the category of a natural resource? Who would have thought that Thailand would consider an 800-year old sunken ship to be natural resource? Certainly not its prospective salvors, that's for sure!

Salvors should be aware of the fact that in Southeast Asia, there may be no such thing as international waters for salvaging shipwrecks. No matter where you happened to have located a sunken ship, you can bet your life that some country will claim that territory. In many cases, several countries may have staked a claim to those waters.

An example of this can be seen in the case of the Paracel and Spratly Islands, Macclesfield Bank and Pratas Shoals. These are all located in the South China Sea and are claimed by no less than six countries – China, Taiwan, Philippines, Vietnam, Malaysia and Thailand (wrecks in these areas are discussed in Chapter 6 on Shipwrecks of Asia). In Southeast Asia, jurisdiction over Pedra Branca (also called Pulau Batu Puteh), lying at the eastern entrance to the Straits of Singapore where some ships have been wrecked, is claimed by both Singapore and Malaysia.

So before investing a great deal of time and money into a salvage operation, it is highly recommended that you first and foremost investigate what jurisdiction or territorial waters the ship in question happens to lie in. Then, you can hopefully both come to a legal salvage agreement with the government having jurisdiction.

In the salvage of the Portuguese prizeship FLOR DO MAR (see the end of this chapter), although the wreck was within the territorial waters of Indonesia, the Malaysian government also laid claim to any artifacts recovered from the wreck on the grounds that they were looted from Ma-

THE THAILAND JUNK

There is nothing like a controversial shipwreck to spruce up the latest newspaper headlines. In this case, it was the question of who owned the salvaged treasures of an 800-year old junk that was discovered in October 1991 in the Gulf of Thailand, some 60 nautical miles south of Samaesan, Thailand

The sunken vessel was initially located by a Thai fisherman who, upon retrieving his nets, brought up bits and pieces of snagged pottery. This location was afterwards disclosed to a Thai navy diver who managed to retrieve some pottery from the wreck but afterwards suffered from the bends (the effects of decompression sickness) due the deep dive (200 feet). Some sample pieces of the recovered pottery were sent to Christie's and were appraised at over US$1,000.

Due to the junk's depth and its antiquity value, the services of Michael Hatcher, the well-known Australian treasure salvager, were called upon. Hatcher agreed to investigate the wreck, so a second salvage operation was undertaken in early 1992 along with a sophisticated salvage vessel, *AUSTRALIAN TIDE*, accompanied by three Thai fishing trawlers.

On the first day on the job, as the divers were recovering the ancient ceramics, the *AUSTRALIAN TIDE* was buzzed by a Thai Naval reconnaissance plane. That day, they recovered about 200 pieces from the junk. As the salvage operation continued on the second day, there was another fly-by made by a naval plane. Another 500 pieces of pottery were recovered on this second day. This second fly-by in two days prompted the salvors to wonder why the Thai navy were suddenly so interested in their operation.

A few days later, two Thai navy warships arrived on the scene and an armed boarding party confiscated all the artifacts and pottery that had been salvaged. The salvors on the *AUSTRALIAN TIDE* were ordered to stop all salvage operations and the Thai warships escorted the Thai fishing trawlers back to the nearby port of Sattahip.

This incident raised an important territorial and jurisdictional issue – was the *AUSTRALIAN TIDE*, 60 nautical miles south of Thailand, in international or Thai territorial waters when the treasure was confiscated by the Thai navy? Were the salvors within their rights in salvaging without the Thai government's official sanction, or did their actions violate Thailand's law of the sea and salvage licensing system? Lawyers are now trying to get this question answered and sorted out so that the salvors can get back their confiscated pottery and resume diving operations.

It is understood that a 12-mile limit is normally claimed as territorial waters. However, countries claiming any natural offshore resources (such as oil, gas) have extended their economic and territorial zone out to 200 miles. In this case, another question that is being debated is whether sunken wrecks along with their cargo qualify as natural resources. Until that question is answered, both the Thai government and the salvors remain in conflict.

PRESERVATION AND EXCAVATION

When out scuba diving on some new and exciting reefs, who knows, you may happen to chance upon a sunken ship – it may even be one of those listed in this book. The choice then will be up to you – should you loot the wreck and risk destroying a precious part of the world's maritime history (not to mention a possible jail sentence and fine if caught) or should you try to have the wreck properly excavated by a reputable team of experienced experts? Please make the right choice, and together we can help preserve Southeast Asia's precious maritime history and hopefully bring to light new and exciting finds from the past.

What should a diver do if he or she happens to chance upon one of these sunken time capsules?

- First, you can disclose the wreck location to a reputable salvage company that will take the necessary steps to legally excavate the wreck. Of course, the diver should sign a contract first for a percentage of the goods in case the wreck in question turns out to have some actionable treasures on board. Maybe the diver will even be able to join in on the excavation (should he wish to) and hopefully learn a bit about underwater archaeology.
- Second, the location of a wreck can also be sold outright to anyone interested enough to pay for it. However, this could get a bit tricky because no one in their right mind would pay for a location without first seeing a sample of some of the wreck's cargo.
- Third, you can try and arrange an agreement with the government himself and hire a team of professionals to excavate the wreck However, this is very costly and time consuming.

lacca by the Portuguese in 1511. Indonesia also claimed jurisdiction of the wreck and any artifacts recovered due to the fact that the FLOR sank in its waters.

This just goes to show that even if salvors comply with salvage regulations, its is still only too easy to get caught up in a tug-of-war between countries claiming jurisdiction over a wreck.

In most cases, the three possible claimants to artifacts recovered from shipwrecks could be as follows:

1. The country whose nationality the ship bore at the time of its wrecking
2. The country in whose territorial waters the ship happened to sink
3. The country claiming nationality of the lost cargo

Searching for the Wreck

Once you have obtained the relevant licenses and organized a salvage crew, you can go out to search for the wreck. By this time, you should have analyzed your research and have a pretty good idea of the approximate resting place of your target. We will now discuss some techniques and equipment used in surveying the sea bed to locate the wreck.

Survey Techniques

With a map of the area in question, you should grid off search areas of about one to two square miles each (the size depends on your personal choice and budget). These areas should be marked out according to priority (for example, area #1, #2, #3) – the most likely final resting place of your ship, second most likely place and so on. In this way, you can start surveying in an efficient and logical manner with the minimum amount of time loss.

In salvage operations, it is most likely that you will be towing a side scan sonar. This is an instrument that allows you to literally map the seabed. In order to successfully map the sea floor with the side scan range, line spacing and overlap must be considered. To ensure that you do not miss any small targets, a side scan range of 100 meters is advised (see Figure 1 below).

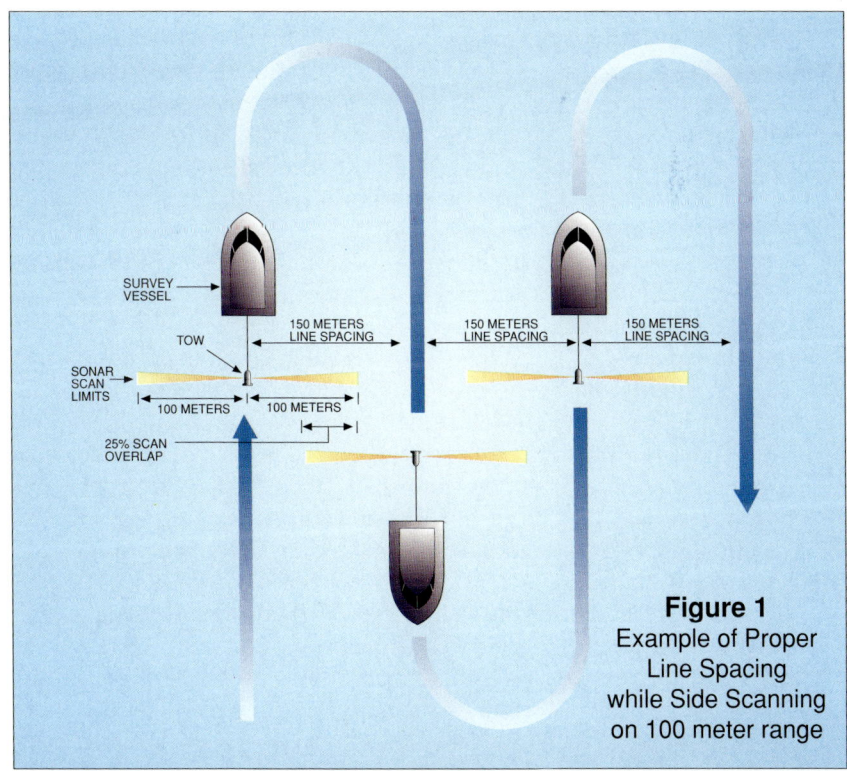

Figure 1
Example of Proper
Line Spacing
while Side Scanning
on 100 meter range

This means that you will be surveying 100 meters *to each* side (port and starboard) of the survey vessel. A higher range will survey a larger area but this results in a smaller paper scale read out which in fact could cause you to miss a small target. For example, while surveying on the 100 meter range print out, a target would be three times larger than one seen on the 300 meter range print out; using the 100 meter range would therefore make smaller targets easier to see.

Line spacing also has to be considered as you will want a certain amount of side scan overlap in order to insure that the sea bed is thoroughly surveyed. A 25% overlap is recommended; for example, 150 meter line spacing on the 100 meter range. That will give you approximately 50 meters overlap on each line.

Positioning systems

Positioning systems tell you exactly where you are in terms of latitude and longitude. There are several different kinds of positioning systems in today's market.

1. **Stand-alone Gobal Positioning System (GPS)**
    Introduced to the general public several years ago, it is now widely used throughout the world. These systems sell for as low as a few hundred US dollars to as high as a few thousand dollars. Some of the cheaper units may not have as many functions as the more expensive ones but are just as or very nearly as accurate when used in the *stand-alone* mode.

    What does *stand-alone* mean? When you are getting your positioning fixes (usually latitude and longitude coordinates) *only* from satellites and without the aid of any other land-based stations, you are positioning in the GPS stand-alone mode. Depending on whether you are stationary or mobile and the number of satellites you are receiving signals from at the time (more satellites means more accurate measurements), positioning can be fairly accurate. If you are moving and receiving good quality signals from four or more satellites, position accuracy will be within 45 feet (15 meters). If you are moving and receiving good signals from only three satellites, position accuracy may not be as good (however, this accuracy increases if you are stationary). At the time of writing, that will give you a working duration of about 18 hours out of a 24 hours period. As more satellites are being added to the sky each year, so the 18 hour working period will therefore increase in time accordingly.

    Some GPS systems have an optional differential mode which makes them very accurate – to within one meter or even centimeters. This is how it works: besides receiving positioning signals from at least two satellites, you are also receiving signals from one land-based station. Because you have entered into your GPS system the exact coordi-

Deploying a marker buoy at a prospective wreck site to be later investigated by divers.

nates of this land-based station (which is stationary and will not move or change position), as long as you are receiving good quality signals from it (and from at least two or more satellites), your positions will be incredibly accurate – usually to within a matter of centimeters.

2. **Differential GPS**

The land base antenna sends signals to the boats receiving antenna by *line of sight*. This means that no physical obstructions should at any time block their field of view, otherwise you lose your signal. The height of the land and boat antennas will also determine the maximum distance you can put between them. The higher your differential base antenna's height (and the boat's receiving antenna) above sea level, the further you can travel out to sea.

For example, assuming that your boat's receiving antenna is at sea level, if your land base antenna is one meter (approximately three feet) high, it would give you a maximum range of four kilometers (2.2 nautical miles). If the land antenna is at 4 meters (13 feet) height, this would equal 8 kilometers (4.3 nautical miles) maximum range; if the antenna is at 10 meters (33.3 feet) height, 12.9 kilometers (7 nautical miles) is the maximum range, and so on.

The only drawback is that this station must have a constant power supply (either AC or DC) while in use. Another problem is that they periodically have to be monitored; as they are expensive, it would be wise to have someone constantly watching them to prevent theft.

3.　**Microwave/fix transponders**

In this case, you are positioning with three (sometimes more) station-ary land-based stations and not using satellites at all. This positioning system is very accurate (to within centimeters). Coordinates are usu-ally received in *eastings* and *northings*.

Here is how it works: first, you must establish and set up your three or more land-based stations (note that the line of sight rule also applies to these transmitting stations). Exact coordinates of these land-based stations are entered into your microwave receiving unit. These stations also require an AC or DC power supply and periodic maintenance. This makes them expensive and so should be guarded against theft.

By now you should have a better idea as to what the different types of positioning equipment are and their accuracy, drawbacks and benefits. All are quite effective and suitable for any offshore surveying operations.

Underwater Detection and Acoustic Equipment
Underwater detection and acoustic equipment are a must for any ocean search and salvage operation. Let's take a brief look at some of these units and instruments.

1.　**Sub-Bottom Profiler**

If your target is buried or if you suspect that it may be buried, one of these would be well worth having. This instrument sends low fre-quency ultrasonic sound waves into the water via transducers. These sound waves penetrate through the sea bed and, upon hitting any buried solid objects, are reflected back up into the transducers, thereby registering the buried object and its depth on a paper read-out. It is usually towed behind the boat, either by floating on the surface or underwater.

2.　**Side Scan Sonar**

Almost all surveying operations have side scan sonars on the project. This instrument, which is normally towed underwater behind the vessel, literally *maps* the sea bed, showing the operator topside a paper printout of the sea bed. A tow fish transmits high frequency sound waves through port and starboard transducers. Upon hitting any unburied objects, a shadow effect is created topside on the ther-mal paper.

As Figure 2 below shows, by measuring the length and range of this shadow (and knowing the height of the tow fish from the bot-tom), the height of the object in question can be determined.

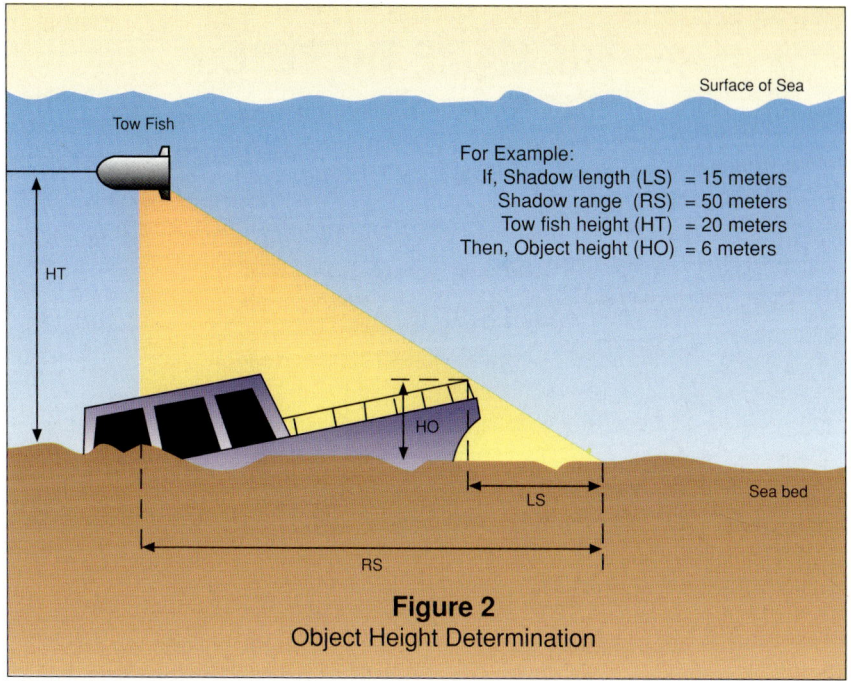

For Example:
If, Shadow length (LS) = 15 meters
Shadow range (RS) = 50 meters
Tow fish height (HT) = 20 meters
Then, Object height (HO) = 6 meters

Figure 2
Object Height Determination

The formula is:

$$HO = \frac{LS}{RS} \times HT$$

(where HO = height of object, LS = length of shadow, RS = shadow range and HT = tow fish height)

3. **Proton Magnetometer**

This instrument is very important in detecting ferrous metals, such as iron or steel, and is usually towed simultaneously along with the side scan sonar. It works by measuring the magnetic field of the earth. However, it cannot detect non-ferrous metals such as gold, silver or brass.

The strength or intensity of the earth's magnetic field is measured in *gammas*. Typically, in the equatorial regions (0° latitude) the measurement is low (20,000); when approaching the magnetic poles, this measurement increases (up to 90,000). Hence, any ferrous metal will upset the earth's normal magnetic field. Therefore, you should *calibrate* the proton magnetometer for a search area so that when the underwater sensor comes near any ferrous metals, its balance will be upset and thereby register a sudden difference in gammas. A north–south surveying direction and vice versa is preferred as this gives the biggest peak-to-peak variation over the object.

THE MARIE THERESE

On November 2, 1871, the 503-tonnage registered French ship MARIE THERESE departed Bordeaux, France for her journey to Saigon, Vietnam. Among other things, the vessel was loaded with thousands of bottles of fine French champagne, wine, clay pipes and some tin ingots. The journey was relatively uneventful until February 29, 1872 when the ship struck a submerged reef on the western part of the Gaspar Straits and immediately started taking on water.

As the vessel was taking on too much water, Captain Moure felt that it was beyond saving and ordered it to be abandoned at once. Having no time to save any of the cargo, the captain and crew departed in the ship's long boats. Somehow, among the confusion of abandoning ship, two of the crew members went missing. After 60 hours in the long boats, the captain and crew were rescued by a passing ship just north of the Thousand Islands group in Indonesia's Java Sea.

In 1990, a French-led salvage group called Matcosub Pte Ltd based in Singapore was awarded a concession license by the Indonesian government to survey and salvage shipwrecks in the Gaspar Straits. At the time, they had no idea that the MARIE THERESE was wrecked in the licensed area. While surveying in May 1991, Matcosub chanced upon the wreckage of the MARIE THERESE southwest of Pulau Lepar in 60 feet of water. Upon initial investigations, divers found thousands of champagne and wine bottles, many still corked and full. This prompted them to have the unidentified wreck researched further. They also called in underwater archaeologists and photographers from France to do a proper archaeological excavation of the sunken vessel. This was the first ever proper underwater archaeological excavation on a sunken ship in Indonesia.

An island (Pulau Ruh) was rented from the Indonesian government for the purpose of building a base camp. Eventually, an archaeology restoration and laboratory treatment room, a photo lab and personnel housing were built. Clearly, no expenses were spared to fund this operation. Unfortunately, this led to the downfall and bankruptcy of Matcosub's Gaspar Straits salvage operation.

A year later, Matcosub had salvaged 5,192 wine bottles, 938 champagne bottles of different sizes, 503 Pernod bottles, 70 Marie Brizard bottles, 3,783 ceramic smoking pipes, 86 tin ingots, 5 empty safes and many other miscellaneous items.

In 1992, Pentagon SA (Matcosub's parent company in France) made up a beautiful auction catalogue that included the sunken ship's history along with many photos, drawings and illustrations. The idea was to bring the restored cargo back to Bordeaux, France and auction it there. The auction did take place. However, due to the massive expenses incurred during salvage and restoration operations, they were unable to cover their costs. To date, the salvage project had cost approximately US$6.5 million. The goods were eventually auctioned in France in 1992 for approximately US$30,000 (of which 50% went to the Indonesian government). Unfortunately, Matcosub went bankrupt shortly afterwards and lost their survey license for the Gaspar Straits area.

4. **Underwater Metal Detectors**

Metal detectors basically work on the same principle, whether underwater or on land. When switched on, a magnetic field is created around the detectors' coil. Should any metal (ferrous or non-ferrous) come within range of this coil, it will upset the coils magnetic field, registering and sounding off the detector.

The detectors' sensitivity varies with the many different brands and also what size coil is in use. Generally, a 12-inch coil should be able to detect an object the size of a 20-cent Singapore coin buried at about 12 to 18 inches and a large cannon at about four to six feet. Again, this detection range may be better or worse depending on other conditions at the time (such as how long the detected object has been buried, its level of deterioration, the type of sea bed sediment and other factors).

The author tests a hand-held underwater metal detector before a dive.

I have only touched briefly on some equipment and techniques used to search for shipwrecks. Keep in mind that there are many other models and equipment on today's market concerning search and salvage operations. Every year, fascinating and advanced new technology and instruments are being introduced to this field. Sophisticated Remotely Operated Vehicles (ROVs), deep diving systems and ultra sensitive electronic detection equipment are becoming more widely used in new and exciting discoveries today that were thought impossible not too long ago.

Some salvage groups recently claimed to have located sunken wrecks covered with tons of mud with the aid of satellites hovering hundreds of miles above the earth's surface. This may sound far-fetched and unbelievable to most people today, but don't be surprised if in the near future this is possible. With the way modern technology has been advancing lately, I think it is safe to say that the "sky is the limit".

In Chapter 6 on Shipwrecks of Asia, you will find a list of over 450 vessels that sank in Southeast Asian waters (parts of Northeast Asia and South Asia are also included) between the years 1511–1890. Where available, the names and places of many of the shipwrecks and dangerous reefs of the region are listed and therefore will be known to divers.

SAFEGUARDING MARITIME HISTORY AND MARINE ARCHAEOLOGY

Pillaging, looting and destroying a sunken wreck is definately not in anyone's best interest. For every shipwreck that gets ravaged, a precious piece of maritime history may likely be lost forever with it. Some of these vessels are virtual time capsules of maritime history and hold the key to the answers of many questions concerning the ships and life on board during the old days of maritime trade.

The wreck in question should be studied by someone who is knowledgeable about maritime history and marine archaeology to see if it is in fact of archaeological importance. The ship's timbers and construction, navigational instruments and other ancient artifacts should be examined to help us all better understand the lifestyles of these ancient mariners. Unfortunately, there are not many qualified underwater archaeologists around. In fact, the sad truth of the matter is that qualified marine archaeologists are far and few between in Southeast Asia.

Some salvage companies do have personnel who have experience in shipwreck excavation (though this does not necessarily qualify them as underwater archaeologists). However, along with girding, tagging, detailed drawings and lots of photographs of articles (before and after recovery), they might be able to do the job at least adequately.

Excavation Equipment

In most cases excavation equipment is needed to recover items from a ship that has been submerged for 100 years or more. The ship will likely be covered over by mud, sand or coral.

- If mud, sand or light coral is covering the wreck, an airlift can be used to remove this. The most common airlift is constructed of a 6, 8 or 12-inch diameter PVC pipe (the length can range anywhere from 6 to 20 feet or more) with a one-inch air hose and valve connected at its bottom end. Compressed air is pumped down to the bottom of the PVC pipe and then flows upwards, thereby causing a suction effect.
- If the wreck happens to rest in shallow water (10 to 40 feet), the salvage ships props can be put to good use in quickly removing mud, sand, or light coral. A mail-box can be constructed and placed behind the propellers that diverts the props water stream in a downward direction. This method of removing sand was commonly used in the shallow waters of the Florida Keys by the Mel Fisher salvage team while searching for the Spanish galleon, *NUESTRA SENORA DE LA ATOCHA*.

- If a shipwreck is buried under several layers of hard coral, excavating it can be a slow and tedious project. The coral must be meticulously dislodged using hand tools or sometimes even an underwater pneumatic jack. Remember that at all times that care must be taken not to damage the wreck's ancient and priceless artifacts. The broken coral can then be removed with an air lift.

The Challenge for Salvors

After considering the above methods, you can now maybe begin to understand some of the many challenges that salvagers and marine archaeologists face during a properly carried out shipwreck excavation. Besides this, they are also often faced with the hindrance of strong currents, zero visibility and dangerous marine species.

Excavating a wreck is a costly, slow and tedious process that could take many months or even years to complete. To date, I can only mention two shipwreck archaeological projects in this region that deserve commendation: one was the salvage of the French vessel *MARIE THERESE* by Matcosub Pte Ltd (Singapore) in the Gaspar Straits, Indonesia in 1991 (see The *MARIE THERESE* above); the other was the archaeological excavation of the lost Spanish galleon *NUESTRA SENORA DE LA CONCEPTION* by Pacific Sea Resources (Singapore) led by William Mathers off Saipan in the Northern Mariana Islands in 1987–88. As far as I'm concerned, these two companies set the precedent for the rest of us to follow! Even though the *MARIE THERESE* salvage was a financial disaster, the painstaking archeological efforts and expertise applied in artifact recovery and preservation were excellent.

SEARCH FOR THE LOST TREASURES OF MALACCA

Speculation about the fabulous wealth that sank with the FLOR DO MAR reached amazing proportions, from upwards of $1 billion to even $80 billion (Skin Diver magazine, March 1992).

In 1511, Admiral Alfonso de Albuquerque sailed from Goa in India to Malacca in a fleet of ships to rescue his captured men and capture the city. One of these ships was the "old and unseaworthy" FLOR DO MAR or "Flower of the Sea".

When Malacca was finally captured after fierce fighting, Albuquerque gave his men three days to sack the city. Afterwards, Albuquerque himself said that these spoils were "The richest treasure on earth that I have ever seen". This rich treasure included more than 60 tons of gold booty of all different shapes and sizes, including gilded furniture and the sultan's throne. Ingots and coinage valued at over 15,000,000 crowns came from the sultan's palace alone. An equal amount of gold was also pillaged from the rich merchants of Malacca, most of whom were murdered or had fled the city. More than 200 chests of diamonds, emeralds, rubies, sapphires and other precious stones were also included in spoils. Also among these treasures were two bronze lion sculptures that were a gift from the emperor of China to the sultan of Malacca and had stood guard over the palace doors.

In December 1511, the FLOR DO MAR and three other vessels loaded with Malacca's treasures began the long sea voyage back to Portugal via Goa. However, they encountered a storm near the northern coast of Sumatra which sent the FLOR DO MAR and two other ships to the bottom with all their riches.

Search for the FLOR DO MAR

In 1989, a group of Australian and American salvors and an Indonesian businessman, Tjetty, entered into a venture to salvage Malacca's lost treasures and formed a company called Southeast Asia Salvage. I myself was one of the divers who worked for Southeast Asia Salvage in the search for the FLOR. According to our research, we had just three clues to go on:

1. The FLOR DO MAR was "lost on a rock or reef on the coast of Sumatra, just opposite the kingdom of Daru". Historical accounts show that

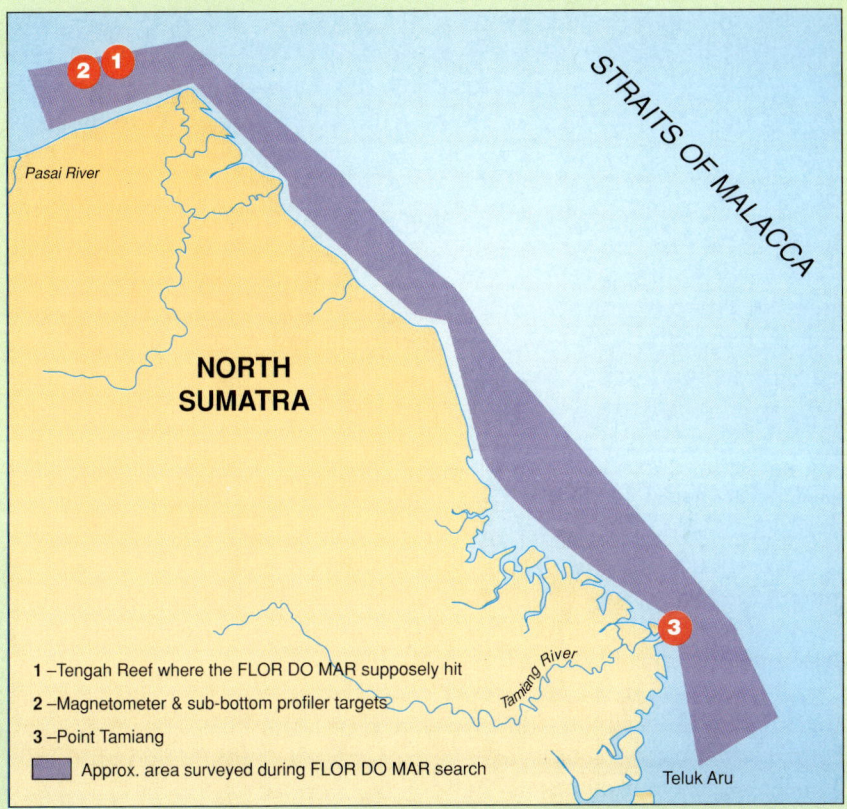

The search area for the FLOR (the shaded portion) covered the entire stretch of coastline from Pasai to Tamiang.

the Daru kingdom (also known as Aru) was at one time located on the northeast coast of Sumatra near what is now known as Point Tamiang.

2. Some survivors from the *FLOR* had managed to get to the Pasem River, though other accounts said the Tamiang River. Known as Pasai on modern charts (there is also a river by the same name), the area is located on the northeastern-most top of Sumatra island. The Tamiang River is located at Point Tamiang, approximately 60 miles south of Pasai.

3. Another clue to the ship's final resting place was that the rock or reef that the ship had hit was "within a cannon shot of the shore" (about one mile).

There are two additional clues: first, if the ship hit on a rock or reef, the water depth couldn't have been more than between 20 to 30 feet, the maximum water depth drawn by the heavily laden *FLOR DO MAR* (even taking into account an amount of swell caused by the storm), and second, this rock or reef should be within a mile (1.6 kilometers) or so from shore.

Based on the above, our two priority survey areas were Tamiang and Pasai. Since they are 60 miles apart, it was decided to survey the entire coastline between these two points up to approximately two miles off-shore. In this way, we were sure that our chances of locating the sunken vessel would increase drastically due to the fact that we were surveying *both* high priority possible wreck sites and also the entire length of coast between the two areas.

Our search began in May 1989 down south in the Tamiang area. For two and a half months, we surveyed this entire area with a side scan sonar, sub-bottom profiler and proton magnetometer, dropping marker buoy's and diving on countless targets (see Chapter 4 for an explanation on the use of these instruments). Each target had to be investigated to confirm whether or not it was a clue to the whereabouts of the *FLOR DO MAR*. As the Taming river delta was heavily silted, many of our magnetometer targets were completely covered by mud. If the target was buried (which was usually the case), the diver then had to do a circle search around the dropped marker buoy with a hand-held underwater metal detector. Once he pinpointed the target with the hand-held detector, these targets had to be dug up manually by the diver with an air lift. Any one of these targets could take from an hour to a few days to uncover, depending on the depth and the hardness of the mud. Usually the divers worked by touch because the underwater visibility was zero and you couldn't even see your hand right in front of your face. Uncovered targets were then brought to the surface (to prevent relocating and digging them up again) and analyzed.

While surveying at Tamiang we recovered several old anchors, a Chinese junk rudder, a steamship shaft with propeller, railroad tracks, airplane

Divers were plagued by poor visibility at Tamiang reef during the search for the FLOR.

Air lifting at the site where the FLOR was believed to be.

parts and many other miscellaneous items. We also dived on a sunken Japanese World War II wreck where I recovered a gas mask and a brass wheel – but not the *FLOR DO MAR*.

By March 1990, when we were absolutely sure that the *FLOR* was not at Tamiang, we began our systematic search north up the coast of Sumatra. By this time, the divers were relieved to leave the Tamiang area – everyone's spirits were low, not to mention that we had all had it up to our necks (literally) with constantly diving and digging in mud. We all knew that the water was much clearer at Pasai (north Sumatra) and looked forward to the change.

Upon reaching Pasai, we built a platform on one of the shallow reefs (Karang Timau) to position and guide the *MINNOW*, our survey boat. We began surveying there on March 8, 1990, and as Tjetty was under pressure from our financiers to start producing artifacts from the *FLOR DO MAR*, he called in the well-known American underwater archaeologist, Bob Marx who said he had information that would lead us directly to the *FLOR*.

Discovery?

On March 25, 1990, while surveying with the sub-bottom profiler about 300–400 meters southwest of Tengah reef (north Sumatra), Marx discovered the existence of a suspicious object that was 10 meters long buried about three to four meters below the sea bed. He believed that this was wood from the *FLOR DO MAR*. We marked the spot and continued our survey, mostly concentrating around this reef.

The following day, another interesting target was found about 200

Blasting mud with a high pressure waterjet gun at the FLOR's *supposed site.*

meters southwest of Tengah reef, this time with the magnetometer. It gave a reading of about 48 gammas. But although we dived on this target with a metal detector, it did not register anything, indicating that the object was buried too deep and out of range for the hand-held detector to pick up. Marx believed that it was ferrous metal from the FLOR DO MAR (a proton magnetometer only detects *ferrous* metals; other metals such as gold, silver and bronze cannot be detected with a proton magnetometer).

It was then decided to dig up and air lift this target out. The water depth was 70 feet to the mud, and each diver spent one hour on the bottom air lifting mud and then had a few minutes decompression stop during ascent at 20 and 10 feet respectively. For the first few feet, the mud was soft and was easily removed with the air lift. But after the first five feet of mud, we came to a layer of clay-mud that was extremely compacted. We first had to physically dig it out with our hands while the air lift sat in the bottom of the hole sucking the loosened mud out. Then, we used a water jet gun to blast the clay-mud free while the air lift sucked it out, but progress was very slow. After an entire week of work, the hole was only 14 feet deep by 10 feet wide – and we still had not dug up any solid evidence of the FLOR DO MAR.

While viewing our sub-bottom profiler records of this area, we could clearly see that there was a very hard layer of rock and sand at 50 feet below the soft mud line. According to Marx, this would be the maximum depth that we had to dig to get to the FLOR, since the 50-foot layer was so hard that nothing could possibly sink below it, not even the heaviest objects made of gold. It was then decided that clam shelling would be the quickest way to dig out this target. This is a recovery technique where a crane (using a grab bucket) from the surface reaches into the sea and digs out the seabed. Further air lifting was abandoned and we concentrated on our survey along the coast with the MINNOW, our survey vessel.

Initially, I named our survey boat MINNOW as a joke about the American television series, *Gilligans Island*. However, it wasn't a joke when we woke up after a storm on the morning of June 5, 1990 and found that the MINNOW had sunk at her moorings! Well, she hadn't completely sunk as the tip of her bow was still bobbing up and down in the rough seas. We made a desperate attempt to save her but to no avail as the weather became rougher. She eventually sank to her watery grave on the seabed.

Unfortunately, the MINNOW had sank with almost US$100,000 worth of survey and positioning equipment on board. We dived that day and recovered all of the lost gear, although most of the electrical equipment was already ruined by the sea water. As it was now pointless to hang around Sumatra, we then headed back to Singapore to regroup and organize a new survey boat, more survey equipment, a crane and barge.

The Final Search

We arrived back on location at the end of July 1990 and clam shelling on the magnetometer target started on August 1. The plan was to dig down until we found some concrete evidence of the FLOR. Then, to prevent damaging any of the precious items from the shipwreck, the divers would then start the slow but safe process of manually air lifting the mud out.

In the end, our magnetometer hole was 50 feet deep (in most spots) and about 100 meters wide. The sub-bottom profiler hole dug did produce some wood fragments but was abandoned at a depth of about 20 feet (width was about 40 to 50 meters). But we never got to the stage of handling any treasure because we never dug up anything concrete – except for two bottles and some wood, we found *absolutely no treasure*! On Tengah Reef we found a few loose ballast stones but nothing more. So, what really happened to all that fabulous treasure? Your guess is as good as mine!

As for the mysterious 48 gamma magnetometer target that we tried to dig up, we may never know what it was. Whatever it was, I feel that it couldn't have been too big an object (possibly weighing 100 pounds or less) due to the rapid rise, peak and fall of the magnetometer gamma readings (it all happened within about 15 to 20 meters at most). Anyway, the size of this unknown object is not really the issue here, the fact is that there was *something* metallic buried there. It's still there today and good luck to anyone who can dig it up. We abandoned the clam shelling op-

The MINNOW being salvaged

Side scan read-out of the hole dug at the FLOR site.

eration on October 29, 1990 and never returned to the supposed *FLOR* site.

Lingering questions still remain about our salvage operation – we certainly did come across a wreck at Tengah Reef but was it really the *FLOR DO MAR*? If it was the *FLOR*, what happened to her treasure? Well, according to some accounts, there was a Sultan in Pasai who suddenly became extremely wealthy soon after the *FLOR* sank. Were his sudden riches pure coincidence or did he in fact salvage most of the treasure of the doomed ship? I leave you to draw your own conclusion.

The GLASS WRECK

In early December 1990 after the search for the *FLOR DO MAR* had been abandoned by Southeast Asia Salvage, we headed for the Gaspar Straits with the work boat *OSAM DRAGON* and a barge in tow.

Tjetty had earlier negotiated with some local Bangka Island fishermen to show us the location of a shipwreck that contained Chinese porcelain and European bottles. (I named this ship the *GLASS WRECK* for its cargo of hundreds of different shapes and sizes of bottles and bundled up sheet glass.) Tjetty was hoping, as one last desperate attempt, that we could salvage something fascinating enough to redeem ourselves and regain attention, interest and more financing from the investors.

As it was December and the monsoon season, the sky was constantly overcast and the weather was rough. This hindered the fishermen in locating the *GLASS WRECK* as they could not see their usual landmarks. The *OSAM DRAGON* being much too large to survey off, I was forced to mobilize the side scan sonar and Gobal Positioning System (GPS) on to the fishermens' small boat. After three days of side scanning, the *GLASS WRECK* was located. But because of rough weather, we were only able to dive on this wreck for two days. During this time, we recovered Chinese porcelain, many European bottles of all different shapes and sizes, two iron English cannons and other miscellaneous items.

Tjetty was very happy with our recoveries. However, the project's sponsors, the Salim Group, withdrew their financing for the *FLOR DO MAR* project. In mid-1991, Southeast Asia Salvage faded into oblivion.

5
WHICH WRECK IS IT?

After you have located a wreck, how do you identify it and assess its age? In most cases, this is a time consuming and difficult task that usually requires the assistance of experts since there are numerous combinations and factors involved in identifying and dating a shipwreck.

This chapter only deals with wooden ships – ships that sank at least a century or more ago. The dating of steel ships is not of our concern here since identification only requires a bit of scraping on the steel hull where the ship's name is welded. Unfortunately, the identification of wooden ships is not quite so easy. After having been below the sea for 100 years or more, wooden wrecks are usually nothing more than a pile of rubble. However, there are exceptions to this, such as in the case of the GLASS WRECK which we located during the search for the FLOR DO MAR. This wreck was sitting up right with its copper-sheathed hull protruding two meters above the seabed. However, I believe that this wreck is an exception to the rule. Its height made it very easy to pick up on the side scan sonar – most other wrecks would not be so easy to find.

In this chapter we will go over a few basic ways of wreck dating and identification so that you will hopefully have some idea of the origin and date of the vessel in question. However, the wreck identification data here

After over 100 years submerged in the sea, a ship's cargo is usually reduced to rubble.

WRECK DISINTEGRATION

Having often spent centuries submerged in the sea, nearly all wooden wrecks will have disintegrated and been reduced to a heap of rubble. Once settled in its final resting place, a ship slowly starts to disintegrate. Wood-boring worms attack the exposed wood, wave action and currents agitate the ship and break up the timbers, and iron fastenings holding the ship together start to rust. After a few decades, the inner decking would have collapsed from the weight of cargo and cannons. Any remaining wood such as on the hull and the lower deck would be already porous from attack by boring worms. After a hundred years, all the exposed wood will have disappeared, leaving just a pile of ballast and cargo.

The rate of disintegration depends on sea temperatures, depth and the water motion. Warmer temperatures, shallower depths and rougher seas accelerate disintegration, while colder temperatures and deeper depths slow down the disintegration process. For instance, a vessel lying at 40 feet depth along a coral reef will be badly battered by wave action and its iron cargo will be seriously oxidized by the higher oxygen content: after 100 years, only a ballast pile may remain to mark the ship's resting place. On the other hand, a wreck in 100 feet of calmer water will probably be better preserved from destructive wave action and oxidation.

However, wrecks can also be protected from disintegration by sand and mud. Wood that is buried in sand or mud is protected from weathering and sea borers, thereby preserving it for a longer time. Copper sheathing also has the effect of preserving wood. When exposed to sea water, copper becomes coated with copper sulfate which repels wood borers and preserves the wood.

Iron items such as anchors and cannons will be subjected to oxidation where air bubbles and dissolved oxygen in the water cause the iron to rust. As mentioned earlier, the rate of oxidation depends on the oxygen content in the sea. If a cannon lies under breaking waves, oxidation will take place very quickly and a cannon can be rusted to almost nothing in 50 years. On the other hand, the iron cannons recovered from the GLASS WRECK were found to be in excellent condition after marine growth was removed – this wreck was at a depth of just over 100 feet. Iron can also become badly sulfated when it is buried under mud in plankton-rich waters and takes on a greyish-silver appearance.

Silver pieces of eight become black and slightly larger after a century in the sea; the silver content is still there underneath a black layer of sulfide coating, although some or most of it may be sacrificed over a period of time. If the silver coins are fused together in a large clump, the outer coins will be corroded while the inner coins should still be in good condition. Also, if silver is in contact with iron or another element of higher valence, electrolytic chemical action will cause it to remain pure silver. Silver ingots will have a coat of black sulfide but will usually not be badly damaged.

Gold still looks as good as new after centuries under the sea – there is never any chemical change to gold no matter how long it is submerged!

is very basic. More detailed dating and identification information can be found in books that specialize in this area. Some books that I would recommend are *The Treasure Diver's Guide* by John S. Potter Jr., *Sunken Treasure – How to Find It* and *The Underwater Dig*, both written by Robert F. Marx. These have more detailed information on shipwreck dating and identification.

Where do you start looking?
Suppose you have located a pile of ballast stones, cannons, some copper sheathing and an anchor on your wreck site. What next? Perhaps you're asking yourself "Is this the wreck that I have been looking for, or is it some other doomed ship that happened to have also foundered in my search area?". These are the questions that you need to ask in identifying wrecks. If you know what clues to look out for in the items and artifacts found on the wreck site, you should be able to make a pretty fair assessment.

If you happen to have the cargo manifest for the particular ship that you are searching for, this would be an invaluable aid in positively identifying the ship. Simply compare the items recovered with your list in hand, and if everything matches up, this would guarantee that it is in fact the ship you are looking for. Even given all the combinations, no other vessel could possibly have the exact same type and number of items as listed on your manifest. Also, goods were bartered, bought and sold from multiple countries and ports of all nationalities, complicating the wreck origin even more.

Check and cross check all of your artifacts and clues against the type of artifacts carried on ships of various nationalities at that period. This is what the proper identification process involves. Then if you really want to positively identify it, get the assistance of an expert.

The following sections guide you in what to look out for when identifying a wreck.

Coinage
Divers should not overlook any round or variously shaped blackened or corroded objects. A general safe rule is to bring up to the surface any object or things of suspicious shape for closer examination. These unidentifiable objects may be encrusted coins, ingots or bars of silver or gold. These treasures are generally worth many times their weight in bullion.

It is possible sometimes to date the wreck from coins or bars recovered. Upon examining these coins or bars, you should at the very least be able to get a better idea as to when the ship sank. For instance, if the coins (or bars) have legible dates on them, what are the latest dates?

Let's say that your wreck has a few thousand coins dated in the 1730s but also has a few hundred coins dated 1750. As 1750 is the latest date found, it is safe to assume that the vessel sank sometime *after* 1750, not before. Alternatively, you might just have happened to find one wreck that had sank right on top of another, and therefore, the cargoes of the two ships could be mixed together. This is a common occurrence, especially on the tracks of major shipping lanes where dangerous reefs are located. In this case, you may even find several vessels virtually stacked right on top of each other!

Oriental Ceramics and Glass
To describe the numerous types of North and Southeast Asian porcelain and ceramics throughout the various countries and dynasties would require an entire book of its own. The field of pottery identification is complicated and highly involved and it is best left to the experts. However, the following table lists the important dates and dynasties when different types of ceramics were made:

CHINA	**A.D.**
Tang (T'ang) dynasty	618–907
Five dynasties	907–960
Song (Sung) dynasty	960–1271
Northern Song dynasty	960–1271
Southern Song dynasty	1127–1271
Yuan dynasty	1271–1368
Ming dynasty	1368–1644
Qing (Ching or Manchu) dynasty	1644–1911
INDONESIA	
Srivijaya empire	600–1200
Majapahit empire	1200–1500
JAPAN	
Heian period	794–1185
Kamakura period	1185–1336
Muromachi period	1336–1568
Momoyama period	1568–1603
Edo period	1603–1868
KAMPUCHEA (Cambodia)	
Major ceramic period	900–1250
KOREA	
Koryo dynasty	918–1392
Yi dynasty	1392–1910
THAILAND	
Sawankhalok ware	1350–1500
Sukhotai ware	1350–1500
VIETNAM	
Early export	1200–1400
Middle export	1400–1600
Late export	1600–1700

There are numerous books that explain in detail just about everything there is to know about North and Southeast Asian ceramics. One easy to understand pocketsize book is *A Guide to Oriental Ceramics* by Elizabeth Wilson. It is written in simple terms that any novice will comprehend. Another excellent book with plenty of photos and illustrations for identifying and dating of ceramics is *The Ceramics of South-East Asia: their Dating and Identification* by Roxanna M. Brown. If Ming and Ching porcelain are your main interest, an absolute must would be *The Hatcher Porcelain Cargoes*, jointly authored by Colin Sheaf and Richard Kilburn – the porcelain photos in this book are excellent.

Some porcelain may even carry dates and names of the country that it was made for. Stacks of oriental ceramics on board would indicate:

1. If an Asian vessel (for instance, a China junk), it could have been bound for any southeast Asian port or west bound to India, Africa or the Middle East.
2. If the vessel was of European origin, it was probably enroute to a Southern Asian port under European control, or a homeward-bound ship which could also discharge cargo along its route at any European controlled ports.
3. An American ship would have been either headed east for the United States or west for Europe.

A cargo of glassware would indicate that the carrier was from Europe, most probably bound for a North or Southeast Asian country, without treasure on board. Glass can be easily dated using scientific techniques (see Bottle Identification and Scientific Dating Methods below).

Wood

In most cases, the only remaining fragments of wood found on wrecks would be found below the ballast buried under sand or mud. All the exposed wood will probably have disintegrated. According to *The Treasure Diver's Guide* by J.S. Potter Jr., the type of wood can give clues as to the ship's nationality:

1. Oak – it took two thousand loads of oak to make one of the larger English East Indiamen ships. American ships and ships of many other nationalities were also built with oak. Spanish *naos* had oak keels and ribs.
2. Cedar – possibly a Spanish galleon which often had cedar planking.
3. Mahogany – it could be of a Spanish ship or Manilla galleon. In the Philippines, local mahogany was used for constructing keels, ribs and planks of Spanish ships.
4. Fir – this was used for masts and spars on the Spanish and Manilla galleons. Ships built in India also used fir. A few EIC ships were built in India, the first as early as 1735.

5. Pine – it could be a Portuguese caravel, carrack or galleon built with Portuguese pine.
6. Teak – Portuguese and Dutch carracks or galleons were built of Indian teak and the Manilla galleons had decks made from teak.

To find out more about what type of ship a wreck once was, look out for the keel. This is a long length of timber that runs along the whole of the ship's bottom. If a sunken ship sits in an upright position on the seabed, chances are that at least part of the keel will be buried in sand or mud and will be more protected than other timbers.

The ship's size can be determined by the length of the keel. According to *The Treasure Diver's Guide* by J.S. Potter Jr., "In 1587, a 400-ton Spanish *nao* had a keel 68 feet long; by 1611, it had been extended to 92 feet". The average measurements of English East Indiamen were as follows:

- 500 tons – 102 feet on the keel and 31 feet broad.
- 600 tons – 125 feet total length, 100 feet on the keel and 34 feet in breadth (width).
- 800 tons – 150 feet between perpendiculars (total length), 116 to 118 feet on the keel and 35 to 36 feet broad.
- 1200 tons – 180 to 190 feet between perpendiculars, length of keel 131 to 144 feet, and breadth between 42 to 47 feet.

BOTTLE IDENTIFICATION

For help in identifying bottles, send enquiries to any of the following addresses. Be sure to include a detailed description and photos of the *side* and *bottom* view of the bottle in question.

1. The British Museum
   Great Russell Street
   London WC1B 3DG
   UNITED KINGDOM

2. National Bottle Museum
   Elsecar Project
   Wath Road, Elsecar
   Barnsley, S. Yorks
   S74 8HJ
   UNITED KINGDOM

3. Old Bottle Club of Great Britain
   2 Straford Avenue
   Elscar
   Barnley, South Yorkshire
   S74 8AA
   UNITED KINGDOM

4. Museum of London
   London Wall
   London EC2Y 5HN
   UNITED KINGDOM

5. Barockmuseum
   0-8105 Moritzburg bei Dresden
   Schloss Moritzburg
   GERMANY

6. Museum des Kunshandwerks
   Leipzig, Grassi-Museum (Museum of Arts and Crafts)
   0-7010 Leipzig
   Johannisplatz
   GERMANY

7. Corning Museum of Glass
   One Museum Way
   Corning, New York 14830-2253
   USA

NO WOOD, NO WRECK!

 If you don`t find any wood, you may not actually have located a wreck at all. This may be hard to believe, but the fact is that if you just find cannons, ballast, anchors and cargo but no wood, it is possible that these could all have been jettisoned from a grounded vessel to lighten her in order to prevent total loss of the ship. For instance, the EIC ship *INGLIS*, dispatched from Canton on November 11, 1821, was grounded on December 11 on Lucipara Shoal in the Bangka Straits, Indonesia. The ship was refloated only after throwing overboard her guns, water, spares and a good deal of private trade, including 5,000 chests of tea. This drastic action to lighten the ship was not all that uncommon (see Chapter 3). So, if upon further investigation, you find no wood on your site, you may actually be at someone's dump site, not a wreck site. (The above wood fragments were recovered from the *FLOR* site.)

Between 1748–1772, all EIC vessels were registered at one size – 499 tons – simply to save money. During this time, any craft registered at 500 tons or more was obliged by law to have a chaplain on board. To avoid this extra expense, shipowners caused their ships to be rated at 499 tons although many of these vessels were in fact of a much higher tonnage.

The chart below shows the difference between the actual tonnage and the chartered tonnage of the ships in the company's service as seen from a comparison of two shipping registers – the Blackwall Yard list and Hardy shipping list.

Ship	Year	Blackwall	Hardy
ROYAL CHARLOTTE	1761	699 tons	499 tons
CLIVE	1762	687 tons	499 tons
THAMES	1764	692 tons	499 tons
DUKE OF CUMBERLAND	1765	692 tons	499 tons
VALENTINE	1767	692 tons	499 tons

The China junks were very large seagoing vessels, some of them having a burthen of up to 600 tons or more. The Siamese junks (of early 1800) were considerably smaller than Chinese junks. Their burthen was from 100 to 350 tons, the average being about 150 to 200 tons.

SCIENTIFIC DATING METHODS

GLASSWARE

The Corning Glass Museum of Corning of New York, USA, has conducted considerable research into methods of identifying and dating glassware. Over time, different methods and minerals have been used to make glassware, and scientific examination can identify the place and date of manufacture of most glassware.

Several years ago, Dr Robert Brill at the Corning Museum developed a method of precisely dating glass recovered from the sea. The length of time under the sea is established by counting the number of layers of the weathering crust of the glass fragment. The findings are generally accurate to within a year or two of the known date of the wreck.

CERAMICS

Developed at the Oxford Research Laboratory in England only a few years ago, thermoluminescence can be helpful in determining the dates of ceramic materials such as dinnerware or building bricks.

Radioactivity from certain isotopes in clay is trapped in until the material is fired in a kiln. The firing releases the electrons in a thermoluminesent glow. When the object cools, the electrons are again trapped but continue to increase with the process of decay. In turn, the number of electrons released increases with the length of time. By measuring the number of electrons remaining in the test object, an approximate date of origin can be established.

ORGANIC MATERIAL

Carbon-dating using radiocarbon 14 (C-14) is a well known method for dating very old objects but it is limited to organic material such as wood, bone, charcoal, peat, shell and plant.

Nuclear physicist W.F. Libby discovered that all organic material absorbs C-14 from the earth's atmosphere until it dies. This absorption then ceases and C-14 disintegrates at a known rate over a period time. By measuring the amount of C-14 remaining in organic material, scientists can determine the length of time that has elapsed since the object died. Only small samples of the item are required for this test. If found in the sea, however, the object should remain wet. Many universities and some commercial laboratories have the facilities for C-14 dating.

Testing normally requires from two to six weeks at an average cost of about US$150.00. The drawback is that for an object dating between 300 and 2,500 years old, there is a plus or minus factor of 150 years. So, if your object is 500 years old, the C-14 test will date it as being anywhere from as little as 350 to as much as 650 years old. As you can see, this test is not very helpful for objects that are not extremely old.

Being an organic matter, wood can be carbon dated (*see* Scientific Dating Methods opposite). This scientific test can be useful in telling you how old the wood recovered from a wreck is.

Sheathing

There were three different types of sheathing for wooden ships. Sheathing was a covering that was placed on the bottom of ships below the waterline to protect the ship. They could be either paint or pitch teredo, lead sheathing (in sheets or strips) or copper sheathing.

Sheathing had been experimented with on many occasions, particularly when the ships were intended for special service in waters in which they would be particularly liable to the attack of boring worms. The warm waters of East Asia are a prime example: sea parasites can devour a ship's hull, cutting years off of its normal lifetime. One sheathing fashion introduced by the English navigator John Hawkyns (1532–1595) was to fix a thick layer of tar and hair over the underwater body and cover it with a layer of softwood planking. This planking was easily stripped off and replaced when it became riddled. It was not until the latter half of the 18th century that copper was tried and found to be far superior to any other substance. It functioned both as a protection against barnacles and sea growths, keeping the ship's bottom clean and increasing its speed.

The English first tried copper sheathing on their Pacific ships in 1767 and by 1783, all English vessels were copper sheathed. The French began copper sheathing their ships too by 1778 and the Spanish in the early 1800s. Lead sheeting with nail holes inside the hull or on top of the ballast would probably date the wreck after 1783. This is when store rooms began to be lined with lead.

The Treasure Diver's Guide by J.S. Potter Jr. has the following guide on sheathing:

- If only wood is found on the bottom of a ship and no sheathing, "it could be either Spanish before 1520, Portuguese before 1580, English before 1760, or French or Dutch before 1780. These were the approximate dates that these countries' vessels began to be sheathed."
- If a one-eighth to one-quarter inch thick lead sheathing is found on a wreck's bottom nailed to the outside of the lower planks, "the ship is probably Spanish between 1520 and 1810 ... Some English vessels were sheathed after 1640."
- If very thin copper sheathing is found underneath the hull, "the wreck is possibly English after 1770, or Spanish after 1810."

Ballast

Ballast was a heavy material, either stone or iron, that was used to stabilize ships. Ballast stones were generally rounded or smooth rocks that were taken from rivers. These stones that had been rolled and tumbled over the years were sought after specifically for ballast because of their smoothness. During rough seas, the last thing that sailors wanted to have was a sharp ballast stone that could pierce the hull.

Ballast can indicate whether a wreck dates before or after 1800. Before 1800, ballast stones were usually small-sized – from golf ball size to football size. Many Spanish *naos* and galleons had smooth round granite known as "egg rock" for ballast – these were a light brown colour. After 1800, iron ingots were generally used for ballast instead of stone.

Chalk was used as ballast on English ships. Silver and gold ore were occasionally piled on top of the ballast and this sometimes left shiny specks on the stones. Old cannons were also used for ballast, two tied side by side, muzzles to breech to prevent unwanted movement. They were placed on top of stone ballast to lower the ship's center of gravity.

Anchors, Chains and Cables

The Treasure Diver's Guide by J.S. Potter Jr. provides the following as a general guide to dating anchors:

- If it is hand forged, it was made before 1510.
- If it was cast in one piece, it was probably made after 1510.
- If there is a rectangular hole penetrating the shank near the top at right angles to the arms and flukes, the anchor is dated before 1820 (a wooden or iron crossbar was fitted into this rectangular hole).
- If it has an iron stock or crossbar, it was made after 1820.
- Anchor flukes shaped like a heart or cloveleaf were usually made before 1700.

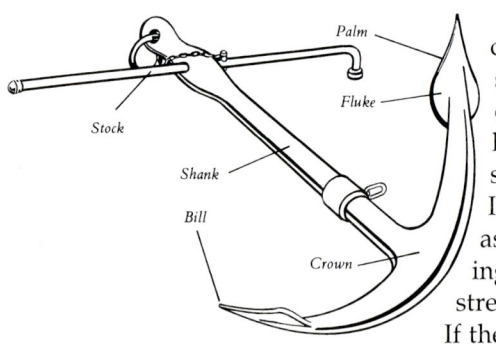

Anchor size does not always give clues as to the ship's tonnage or size since all sailing vessels had more than one anchor. In fact, the larger ships had as many as six anchors of various sizes. For example, English East Indiamen commonly carried as many as five or six anchors, usually consisting of a sheet, best bower, smaller bower, stream and kedge anchor.

If the shank's length is less than nine feet, the ship was probably small, registering less than 400 tons with a total length of not more than 100 or so feet. The larger galleons, frigates and warships (over 400 tons and over 100 feet in length) had anchors over 15 feet long and 12 feet from fluke to fluke. Between 1600 and 1800, the size and shape of large anchors varied very little. English anchors can be identified due to a 1684 decree that *the Broad Arrow* and the anchorsmith's mark must be "cut deep" in English anchors.

Up to the early 1800s, anchors were suspended from rope cables. Finding an anchor chain also helps in determining the age of the wreck since these were used after 1815.

Cannons and guns

Weaponry such as cannons and guns were an essential part of sailing ships that plied the trade routes. Since these ships were usually heavily laden with rich cargoes, they were a target for pirates and as such carried both heavy and light weapons for defence.

Being made of metals such as iron or brass, cannons are sometimes among the more easily found items in wrecks. Their longish shape also makes them easier to find on the seabed and their iron content can be detected by a proton magnetometer. If you come across a wreck that has lots of cannons but no cargo on it at all, it could very likely be a warship: generally, warships of all nations were forbidden to carry cargo of any description.

Although most iron cannons are likely to be badly oxidized, they are often a valuable aid in identifying a wreck. Breech marks on cannons can establish the nationality and date of wreck. Detailed discussion of this is beyond the scope of this book. *The Treasure Diver's Guide* by John S. Potter Jr. has a comprehensive chapter on this.

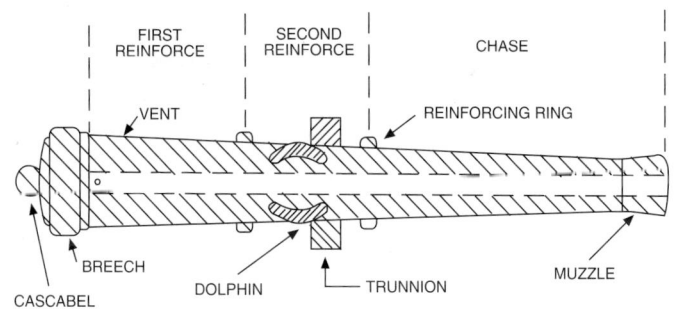

Among the more common guns and cannons carried were the following:

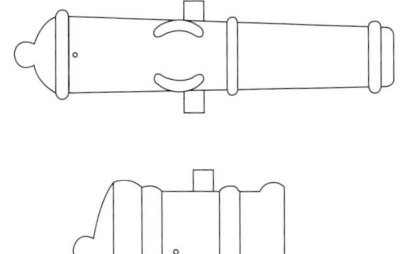

1. Pedrero – Fired stone balls only. Cast in iron or bronze. Used on all European ships between 1540–1700.

2. Mortar – short and fat in shape with a large circumference. Heavy weight of up to several tons. Used for firing mortar bombs from the late 1500s to the 1800s.

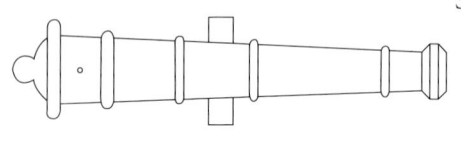

3. Cannon – heavy weight for its length (5 to 7 feet long, one-and-one-quarter to two-and-a-half tons). Made of cast iron and bronze. Most guns found in wrecks dating after 1600 are cannons. Nearly all cannons had markings which are useful in identification.

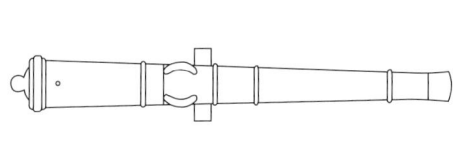

4. Saker – a long range and relatively accurate early gun with a long and slender barrel. Could weigh up to 2,100 pounds and was cast in bronze or iron. Used from 1515 to after 1800 by the Spanish, English and other nationalities as secondary armament on frigates and warships.

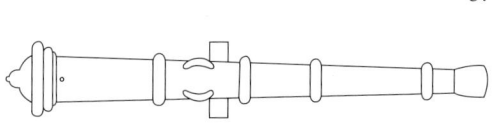

5. Culverin – heavy weight and thick barrel. Length was 11 feet or more with a weight of 2,400 to over 7,000 pounds. Cast in bronze or iron. Used from the early 1500s to 1800s by the Spanish, French and English.

Just because a wreck yields a Portuguese, Dutch or English cannon does not necessarily mean that the vessel is of that origin. Cannons were bought, traded and sold by many nations. After boarding prizeships, pirates looted and kept anything of value, including cannons. The cannons could be later sold or used against enemy ships.

The following are examples of the number and types of guns commonly carried by ships of various nationalities through the centuries:

1515 – a 250-ton nao carried:
    1 demiculverin of 3,200 pounds or 1 cannon of 4,200 pounds
    2 sakers, one of 2,000 pounds and the other of 1400 pounds
    1 falconette of 1,200 pounds
    10 lombards
    24 versos

1702 – *HMS PEMBROKE* (two-decker warship) carried:
20 24-pounder cannons (or demicannons)
2 12-pounder cannons
2 3-pounder cannons
20 demiculverins
10 sakers

1720 – Spanish 776-ton warship *CONQUISTADOR* carried:
26 18-pounder cannons
28 12-pounder cannons
10 8-pounder cannons

1784 – VOC warship *UTRECHT* (arrived in Malacca in 1784) carried:
68 guns on board

1801 – 800-ton EIC ships were armed as follows:
20 18-pounder cannonades (each 6 feet long weighing 26 cwt.)
2 18-pounder cannonades as stern chasers (weighing 30 cwt.)
10 18-pounder carronades (3 feet 6 inches long weighing 11 cwt.)

According to *The London Evening Post* (May 11, 1769), EIC vessels carried an average of 26 guns each. However, larger ships in the China trade after 1784 carried heavier armaments, particularly during the Napoleonic wars with France.

Projectiles
Cannon balls are often found with cannons. They can be solid iron shots, stone balls or even hollow iron shots. The number of rounds (cannon balls or other projectiles) for every gun carried varied depending on the country and the situation at the time.

By 1800, all EIC vessels, no matter what size, were supposed to carry at least 30 rounds for every gun or carronade on board. An inventory of stores for a 500-ton ship in 1804 includes the following items: 400 round shot, 100 double-headed bar shot, 40 grapeshot, and 56 barrels of gunpowder. At that time, the average 500-ton EIC ship carried 16 12-pounder carronades as well as smaller arms.

Among the projectiles likely to be encountered at a wreck site are stone balls (sometimes coated with lead), lead balls, cast iron balls, bar shot or doublehead, chain shot, explosive projectiles, grapeshot, carronade shot, flaming shot, unusual bar shot and mortar projectiles. Detailed descriptions of these are found in *The Treasure Diver's Guide* by John S. Potter Jr.

Light Weapons
Light weapons can also indicate the age of the wreck. For instance, medieval weapons such as spears, lances, shields and breastplates were among

the weapons carried by the early Europeans to the East and were used up till the end of the 1500s. Muskets were used after 1540 and pistols and carbines were used after 1660. Expert advice from an old weapons specialist is important in dating weapon artifacts found in such wrecks.

EIC vessels carried netting and small arms for defence against boarding. For example, a 550-ton ship in 1806 was expected to have boarding netting which could be run up "half mast high", made of one and a half inch rope and strengthened in three horizontal chains. The vessel was also to carry "a stand of arms and cutlass for every man on board, and also twenty boarding pikes". Weapons were usually kept in chests, appropriately known as arms chests.

1804 – the inventory for a 500-ton ship carrying 50 men included:

2 arms chests	25 pistols
6 iron musketoons	50 cutlasses and scabbards
50 muskets	25 pole axes
50 bayonets	30 hand grenade shells
50 boarding pikes	5 half barrels of musket powder
20 scabbards	1 drum of powder

Other clues
Other artifacts can also help in assessing the age of the wreck.

- Navigational instruments such as astrolabes, quadrants and octants can indicate age as they were used until the mid 1700s. The sextant (originally an octant with an arc of one-eighth of a circle) was invented in 1731. It was enlarged to one-sixth of a circle in 1757.
- Copper pumps and salt water distillers appeared on Spanish vessels after 1550. Steam pumps replaced hand pumps for bailing out the hold of ships in 1788.
- The *perulera* was a copper powder bucket used after 1769 on Spanish ships as a container for black powder. It was about 18-inches tall, a foot wide at the bottom and with a narrower 6-inch diameter at the top.
- Electrical lighting was first used on board ships in 1880 and became standard on most ships around 1900. By this time, however, the era of wooden sailing ships had come to an end as they were replaced by steam-powered ships.

TREATMENT OF RECOVERED ARTIFACTS

Once artifacts from wrecks are brought up to air again, it is absolutely vital that they are properly treated, preserved and stored to ensure that they do not disintegrate.

Once the recovered items are brought to the surface, they must be immediately submerged in a fresh water bath or (depending on the object) in a special solution bath to prevent further deterioration. After soaking for a predetermined amount of time, the next step could be to heat the item in a special oven with hydrogen gas, allowing it to dry and then coating it with a special protective coating. For instance, wood has to be treated with polyethylene glycol, a wood preservative that drives out moisture and strengthens the fibers, otherwise it will just crumble away.

There are numerous other combinations of treatment depending on the object type. Ceramics just need to have a fresh water bath but if there is any coral growth on them, then they will need special care in removing the coral without damaging the porcelain. Silver that has a black sulfide coating is treated with electrolysis and gold just needs a rinse with fresh water to look as good as new.

On parting note, I leave you with this thought. An iron cannon brought to the surface and left exposed to the elements will disintegrate to practically nothing within a few months. If you don't have the proper sized storage tank to treat it, it's better to leave it on the sea bottom where you found it! You can easily tell the difference between an iron cannon and a bronze cannon – the iron cannon will be totally covered with thick marine growth while the bronze cannon will have hardly any growth on it at all. (In the picture below, this 18th century iron English cannon recovered from the *Glass Wreck* was found to be in good condition after the coral growth had been chipped away, due to the depth at which it had lain.)

6

SHIPWRECKS OF ASIA

This chapter lists over 450 documented shipwrecks along the trade route in Asia between 1511 through to the late 1800s. Readers should realize that these are by no means *all* the ships that were wrecked or lost in this region. That would be an impossible task. Each day that I spent researching in the National Library in Singapore, I would find at least half a dozen new wrecks to add to my list. Finally, there came a point and time where I had to call it a day. Had I not done that, this book would never have been published!

Many of the wrecks listed may be of interest to the underwater archaeologist though most will be of little or no interest to a treasure salvor due to the perishable cargo carried (such as silk, cotton, coal or tea). I have listed these wrecks mainly for identification purposes in case the modern day salvor should happen to chance upon them while searching for an-

An 18th century map of the East Indies used by the Europeans who contributed greatly to enhancing trade in the region. Of the thousands of sailing vessels richly laden with cargo that traversed this region from the early 1500s onwards, many disappeared without a trace while others sank in identifiable regions.

other ship. However, let us not forget that most ships, if not all, often carried some kind of strong box with cash in it in the captain's room. Not only that, the crew and passengers (if any), would have had their personal effects with them also. A good rule if you have the time is to check any interesting wrecks that you come across.

Southeast Asia is a large region with many countries, some of which have thousands of tiny islands in their archipelago chain. As an aid to locating some of these islands, I have in some cases listed their coordinates (latitude and longitude) and indicated nearby large islands or landmarks. In addition, pictures of old maps and a modern map of Indonesia showing its many seas and islands should help readers to put locations into context.

Although this book aims to principally cover Southeast Asia, I have also included other countries in South Asia and in Northeast Asia as these made up the trade route from East to West. The territorial waters of countries and the seas included in this chapter are as follows:

BANGLADESH
BORNEO
CHINA
INDIA (Andaman and Nicobar Islands)
INDONESIA (Ambon, Bali Sea, Banda Sea, Bangka and Gaspar Straits, Carimata Strait, Celebes Islands, Flores Sea, Halmahera Sea, Java Sea, Madura, Makassar Strait, Moluccas, Riau Archipelago, Sumatra, Sumba Island, Sunda Straits, Ternate and Timor Sea)
JAPAN
MALAYSIA (Straits of Malacca, Johor Straits and River and East Coast of Peninsular Malaysia)
MYANMAR
NEW GUINEA
NORTH CHINA SEA
PHILIPPINES
SOUTH CHINA SEA (Paracel Islands, Pratas Shoals, Spratly Islands and Other parts of the South China Sea)
TAIWAN
VIETNAM

Where there are two or more conflicting accounts of the same ship, these are marked ‡. Where the original records show possible misspellings in names or locations, these are indicated by a (?). Readers should take note that misspellings do frequently occur in many old records.

Definition of terms and abbreviations used:

Year   This is the year that the vessel was wrecked, lost or reported missing.

East Indies	Term used by Europeans when referring to Southeast Asia.
EIC	English East India Company
HMS	His or Her Majesty's Ship (English)
VOC	*Vereenigde Oost-Indische Company* (the Dutch United East India Company)
SEI	Swedish East Indiaman
PEI	Portuguese East Indiaman
P&O	Pacific and Orient Line, a British shipping company

BANGLADESH

Located at the northernmost tip of the Bay of Bengal, Bangladesh is virtually surrounded by India, with Myanmar (Burma) sharing part of its border to the east. The country's heart is the Ganges River which flows from Tibet into India, snakes across Bangladesh and finally flows out into the Bay of Bengal. Bangladesh was formerly known as and was also a part of Bengal, a state in India.

1. **1648 –** *BRAK*, Dutch East Indiaman (tonnage and captain unknown), arrived in Batavia on July 30, 1640. Eight years later on August 10, the ship was wrecked in the Ganges River.
2. **1670 –** *HAPPY ENTRANCE*, EIC ship that was lost in November in the Bay of Bengal while on route from Bengal to England. The ship supposedly had a cargo of precious stones on board.
3. **1672 –** *LOOSDUINEN*, Dutch East Indiaman of 840 tons (captain unknown), arrived in Batavia on July 17, 1669. Three years later on September 20, the ship was wrecked in the Ganges River. The cargo of 204,000 florins was mainly lost.
4. **1674 –** *OSDORP*, Dutch East Indiaman of 448 tons, Captain Pieter Dirksz Haan, arrived in Batavia on July 1, 1671. Three years later on December 5, the ship was wrecked in the Ganges River.
5. **1679 –** *WESTERVERLD*, Dutch East Indiaman of 500 tons (captain unknown), arrived in Batavia on January 19, 1676. Three years later on May 23, the ship was wrecked in the Ganges at Bengal.
6. **1690 –** *DEN HELDER*, Dutch East Indiaman of 578 tons (captain unknown), was wrecked in the Ganges River.
7. **1694 –** *JAMES AND MARY*, English East Indiaman, lost on a shoal near Tunbolee Point, Hugli River while on a voyage from Bengal to England. This shoal today is known as James and Mary Shoal. It is rumoured that the ship had treasure on board.
8. **1698 –** *GRACEDIEU*, EIC ship that was lost in the Bay of Bengal during its journey from Bengal to England. The vessel was supposedly lost with a cargo of 73,294 Spanish reals of eight.
9. **1730 –** *JOHANNA*, Dutch East Indiaman of 550 tons, Captain Hendrik

van Beek, arrived in Batavia on February 14, 1730. Later that year, the ship was wrecked on the Ganges River.

10. **1769** – LORD HOLLAND, EIC ship that was lost in the Hoogley River during passage from Bengal to England. Vessel was rumoured to have had specie on board.

11. **1773** – LORD MANSFIELD, EIC vessel of 499 tons, Captain William Fraser, departed England on December 24, 1772 on her maiden voyage to the East Indies. On September 7, 1773, the ship was lost on the Bengal River.

12. **1779** – STAFFORD, EIC ship of 804 tons, Captain George Hutchinson, departed England for its third voyage on May 27, 1778. On August 29, 1779, the ship was lost on the Bengal River.

13. **1781** – HINCHINBROOKE, EIC ship of 528 tons, Captain Arthur Maxwell. On March 13, 1781, it sailed on its maiden voyage from England to the East Indies. The vessel was lost in the Hoogly River on April 10 in the same year.

14. **1782** – EARL OF DARTHMOUTH, EIC ship of 758 tons, Captain David Thomson, departed from England for her maiden voyage to the East Indies on June 3, 1780. The vessel was lost on Carnicobar Island (Bay of Bengal) on June 24 on its homeward voyage.

15. **1784** – MAJOR, EIC ship of 755 tons, Captain Arthur, which sailed from Portsmouth (England) on February 6, 1782 for the coast (Bengal) and China. The vessel was blown up at Culpee (the mouth of the Hoogley River) by an explosion on board on April 23, 1784.

16. **1792** – PESOUTON, American brig later sold to an Indian company, foundered in the Bay of Bengal. There were some survivors.

17. **1809** – ASIA, EIC ship of 820 tons, Captain Genry P. Tremenheere, sailed from England on September 17, 1808 for its fifth voyage. On June 1, 1809, the vessel was lost in the Bengal River.

18. **1823** – SWALLOW PACKET, EIC ship of 345 tons, was launched at Bombay (India) in April 1777 and sailed the seas until she was wrecked on a shoal in the Hoogley River in June 1823.

19. **1845** – HARLEQUIN, vessel of unknown origin that was lost on the Sandheads, Hougli River while on route from China to England. Rumour has it that the vessel had specie to the amount of US$750,000 on board. A later salvage attempt by divers proved unsuccessful due to strong currents.

20. **1858** – CORNELLA, sailing barque of unknown origin that was lost in February about one to two days sail out of Rangoon, Burma. The ship was headed to Singapore when she capsized on a sand bank. Silver valued at 22,000 reals was rumoured to have been lost with the vessel.

21. **1864** – PERSIA, Indian-owned steamship of 860 tons, foundered in a cyclone in the Bay of Bengal.

22. **1867** – THUNDER, steam vessel of unknown origin which departed

from Pinang, Malaya on October 27 and was not heard of again. It was presumed lost in the Bay of Bengal. Some say that treasure valued at £50,000 was on board.

23. **1879** – *AVA*, British India Steam Navigation Ship of 2,300 tons, was run down and sunk by the *BRYNHILDA* in the Bay of Bengal.

BORNEO

The island of Borneo contains states from three countries: Kalimantan, Indonesia which covers about two-thirds of the island; the East Malaysian states of Sarawak and Sabah that cover just under one-third of the island; and the Sultanate of Brunei located between Sarawak and Sabah, an oil-rich country that has an area of 5,770 sq. km. (2,228 sq. miles).

1. **1608** – A Portuguese ship (name unknown) was wrecked on a sandbank off the mouth of Tanjong Prangi (Feringhie?) off Rijang, Sarawak. The people of Rijang brought the shipwrecked victims to Brunei, where they were well treated by the Sultan of Brunei. One of the shipwreck survivors was known as Father Pereria. After some time, a Macau ship arrived and took the survivors back to that port. Father Pereia was later shipwrecked again when he went back to the Philippines.

2. **1634** – *GOUDEN LEEUW*, Dutch East Indiaman of 400 tons (captain unknown), arrived in the Indies (Batavia) on November 19, 1629. She remained sailing in the Indies and five years later was wrecked on an unknown reef off Borneo.

CHINA

By far the most populous and largest country in Asia. China has a land area of 9,596,960 sq. km. or 3,705,386 sq. miles. It has over 1,500 miles of coastline and numerous offshore islands. The two major rivers of China are the Hwang Ho (Huang He) and the Yangtze (Iang-Tse or Chang Jiang), the world's seventh and third longest respectively.

1. **1541** – Junk in the fleet of the Chinese pirate Coja Acem, was lost in September (?) during a sea battle at Ilheu de Sumbor (located on the China coast opposite northern Taiwan). Ship was presumed fully loaded at the time of loss.

2. **1542** – Portuguese ship under the command of Antonio de Faria was shipwrecked in August at the Iang-Tse (Yangtze) river. The ship was assumed to have had a rich cargo as it was homeward-bound from an expedition to Chinese temples at the time.

3. **1587** – *SAN MARTIN*, China trading *patache*, was broken up on the coast of Canton. She had a fortune in silver money on board. The crew and money were saved. The ship was afterwards burned by the Chinese.

4. **1598** – *SAINT LUIS*, Spanish armada ship, Captain Agv D. Palacio (part of a fleet under the command of Louis DasMarinas), was on a voyage from Philippines to Cambodia. It was stranded on October 3rd and 1,945 men were lost.

5. **1598** – *ALMIRANTA*, Spanish armada ship (part of a fleet under the command of Louis DasMarinas), was on a voyage from Philippines to Cambodia. The ship was lost trading off Canton. It had on board a small fortune in treasure.

6. **1598** – *CAPITANA*, Spanish armada ship (part of a fleet under the command of Louis DasMarinas), was on a voyage from Philippines to Cambodia. The ship was lost trading off Canton. She had on board a small fortune in treasure.

7. **1617** – *NINA CHRISTINA*, lost off the coast of China.

8. **1619** – *UNICORN*, EIC ship of 700 tons, was lost on the south China coast during this year. Afterwards, the English crew members were held prisoner by the Portuguese in Macau.

9. **1627** – *DOMBURG*, Dutch East Indiaman of 100 tons, Captain Jaspar Klaas, arrived in the Indies (Batavia) on March 13, 1627. The ship remained in the Indies and was burnt in the Chincheu river .

10. **1627** – *OUDERKERK*, Dutch East Indiaman of 100 tons, Captain Jouke Piersz, arrived in the Indies (Batavia) on April 18, 1627. The ship remained in the Indies and six months later on October 12 was lost near Amoy, China while fighting the Portuguese.

11. **1631** – *BEVERWIJK*, Dutch East Indiaman of 160 tons, Captain Marten Hendriksz, arrived in the Indies (Batavia) on January 27, 1627. The ship remained in the Indies and four years later on October 22 was wrecked on the coast of China.

12. **1633** – *SLOTEN*, Dutch East Indiaman of 100 tons, Captain Dirk Gerritsz Krul, arrived in the Indies (Batavia) on January 27, 1627. According to one source, the ship was lost six years later on October 7, in the Chincheu river on the coast of China. However, another source says it was lost near Amoy on February 5, 1629.

13. **1633** – *BROKERHAVEN*, Dutch East Indiaman of 100 tons, Captain Marten Jansz Proost, arrived in the Indies (Batavia) on October 22, 1629. The ship remained in the Indies and four years later on October 22, it was destroyed by fire in the Chincheu river.

14. **1647** – *JONKER*, Dutch East Indiaman (tonnage and captain unknown), arrived in the Indies (Batavia) on December 6, 1645. The ship remained in the Indies and two years later was wrecked off Wangkang on 21 October 1647.

15. **1650** – *WITTE DUIF*, Dutch East Indiaman of 380 tons (captain un-

known), arrived in the Indies (Batavia) on March 8, 1648. The ship remained in the Indies and two years later was wrecked on the coast of China.

16. **1651 –** *GOES*, VOC ship of 460 tons (captain unknown), arrived in the Indies (Batavia) on July 1, 1655. Ten years later on March 7, the ship ran ashore at the coast of Quinam.

17. **1652 –** *KOE*, Dutch East Indiaman of 360 tons (captain unknown), arrived in the Indies (Batavia) on June 6, 1647. Five years later on July 20, the ship was lost on the coast of China.

18. **1655 –** *VLEERMUIS (GULDEN)*, Dutch East Indiaman of 150 tons (captain unknown), arrived in the Indies (Batavia) on November 24, 1652. Three years later on September 26, the ship was wrecked on the reefs of the "Vuile Eiland" in the Pescadores (off the China coast) on December 31.

19. **1659 –** *GEELMUIDEN*, Dutch East Indiaman of 202 tons (captain unknown), arrived in the Indies (Batavia) on August 20, 1658. In the following year, the ship was wrecked while sailing to Canton.

20. **1663 –** *ANKEVEEN*, Dutch East Indiaman of 283 tons, Captain Barend Joachimsz, arrived in the Indies (Batavia) on May 30, 1661. Two years later on February 22, the ship was wrecked off the coast of China. The crew were saved.

21. **1667 –** *JONKER*, Dutch East Indiaman of 200 tons (captain unknown), was wrecked on the rocks of the Hytanse Islands on December 17. Of the ship's crew, 33 men drowned and 13 survived.

22. **1683 –** *HUIS TE VELSEN*, Dutch East Indiaman of 506 tons, Captain Kornelis Jansz de Zeeuw, was wrecked at Domar Islands on January 24.

23. **1735 –** *ALBLASSERDAM*, VOC ship, was wrecked off the China coast during its homeward-bound voyage. The vessel had a cargo of Chinese porcelain on board.

24. **1772 –** *RYNSBURG*, Dutch East Indiaman, foundered off the China coast in July. On August 1, five men from this ship arrived at Canton and reported that while their ship was at anchor during a typhoon on July 17, she foundered in 15 fathoms of water. The ship was deeply laden. With all her ports open she took in a lot of water. These five men were cast on the shore near the Mandrin's Cap, from which place they were afterwards brought to Canton. They were the only survivors.

25. **1802 –** *FERROLENA URCA*, Spanish supercargo of 1,200 tons, was lost in September of this year on a voyage from Manilla bound to Canton. The ship met bad weather and, neglecting the lead, was cast on the shore in Kaptchee Bay on the east coast of Kwangtung not far west of Swatow. The people on board were saved but without food, clothes or arms to defend themselves or the ship, the wreck was plundered by the villagers day after day. The Spanish asked for the help of the

English Committee who dispatched the ship COROMANDEL to assist. In all only 66,500 Spanish dollars were salvaged – 8,000 being the flat salvage settlement plus two percent of the silver salvaged. She initially had on board a lading of $850,000 in silver. There is a report that divers later salvaged the remainder of the treasure.

26. **1802** – MODESTE, HMS warship, was ordered to stand–by off Whampoa, rendezvous and transfer her treasure to the English East Indiamen ALBION (as ships of war were not permitted to pass the Bogue). While it was in the course of transfer to the ALBION, the MODESTE was discovered to be on fire. The ship was then scuttled in port in order to save the bullion. Out of 433 chests, 177 had not yet been transferred (136 being in the lower hold) and was later rescued by divers. The 120 chests in the gun room had suffered from fire damage.

27. **1802** – NAUTILUS, ship from Calcutta, was struck on September 15th by a strong gale while entering the Lema Channel (Canton River). The gale increased in strength, causing the vessel to be blown and smashed to pieces on one of the rocky islands northward of the channel. Only one officer and a few of the crew survived.

28. **1815** – WYNDHAM, ship of Calcutta, was totally lost in the Canton River on Brunswick Rock during this year.

29. **1817** – MARQUIS OF CAMDEN, English East Indiaman 1,200 tons, was anchored in the Canton River on September 8 when her main topmast was struck by lightning which set the ship on fire.

30. **1819** – MYSORE, Indian-owned vessel of 777 tons, was wrecked in China.

31. **1825** – ROYAL GEORGE, English East Indiaman of 486 tons, early on the morning of December 24, was discovered to be on fire while at her mooring at Whampoa. In a short time, the ship was a total loss. No lives were lost but none of the 18 officers or 127 seamen on board had time to save anything but the clothes they had on their back. Fortunately for the EIC, the ship's import cargo had already been unloaded.

32. **1825** – LACKASSAR, English merchant vessel, was wrecked on the coast of Hainan sometime during March. The shipwrecked crew and passengers were sent on a China junk from Macau to Canton.

33. **1836** – JAMSETJEE JEEJEEBHOY, Indian-owned vessel, wrecked off Quilon, China.

34. **1873** – NINA, English steamer lost off Hong Kong.

35. **1875** – JAPAN, American steamship wrecked near Swatow.

36. **Year unknown** – ELLEN RODGER, a China tea clipper, was wrecked off the coast of China.

INDIA

The world's seventh largest country, extending from the Himalayas through the Tropic of Cancer to the warm waters of the Indian Ocean at 8 degrees north. The total land area is 3,287,590 sq. km. (1,269,338 sq. miles). This diamond shaped land mass has the Arabian Sea to the west and the Bay of Bengal to its east.

I have not listed all the wrecks in the Indian subcontinent as this could take another book. Instead, I have concentrated on the Andaman and Nicobar Islands which lie on the trade routes and are closest to Southeast Asia.

Andaman and Nicobar Islands
The Andaman and Nicobar Islands in the southern part of the Bay of Bengal became part of India in 1950.

1. **1583** – Portuguese nao (name unknown), bound from Malacca to Goa (India) was wrecked on a shoal off the Nicobar Islands. Fifty people were drowned and 300 others managed to get on shore. A party was sent off to Malacca in the only surviving boat to seek help. A few weeks later when a ship returned to the Nicobar islands, none of those left behind could be found; cannibals from the Andaman and Nicobar island group had carried them off. Some gold and jewels were lost in the wrecking of this vessel.
2. **1606** – On November 19, a fleet of Dutch ships arrived at the Nicobar Islands. In the night, they sent three boats and set fire to a Portuguese ship (name unknown) and two frigates. The Malays looted them before they sank.
3. **1682** – *EARL OF DARTMOUTH*, English East Indiaman of 758 tons, lost at or near the Nicobar Islands.
4. **1815** – *ATHENA*, English brig, Captain Daniels, was wrecked on a reef off Preparis Island in the Andamans on August 10 of that year. The following day, 18 men were sent out on two small rafts to try and bring back help for the captain and crew remaining on the island. On August 13, a passing English vessel, *JAMES DRUMMOND*, noticed a signal flag and sent their long boat to rescue Captain Daniels and eight men from the island. The 18 men that were sent to search for help on the two rafts were never seen again.

INDONESIA

Indonesia is the world's largest archipelago with a total of 13,677 islands (less than 6,000 of which are inhabited). These islands are scattered over an enormous area of tropical seas. However, three-quarters of the area covers the five main islands of Sumatra, Java, Kalimantan (southern Borneo),

Sulawesi (formerly called Celebes) and Irian Jaya (the western end of New Guinea). Indonesia's total land area is 1,904,570 sq. km. (735,354 sq. miles).

Ambon
Ambon Island is located at latitude 3 degrees and 40 minutes south, longitude 128 degrees and 10 minutes east. It lies south of the southwest end of Seram island.

1. **1622** – *EENDRACHT*, VOC ship of 700 tons (captain unknown), arrived in the Indies (Batavia) on March 22, 1620. The vessel remained in the Indies and was wrecked on the west coast of Ambon on May 13, 1622.
2. **1642** – *MAASTRICHT*, Dutch East Indiaman of 600 tons (captain unknown), arrived in the Indies (Batavia) on August 4, 1642. The ship was lost when it was sailing from Malabar to Batavia.
3. **1645** – *ROEK*, Dutch East Indiaman of 200 tons (captain unknown), first arrived in the Indies (Batavia) on April 25, 1639. The ship remained in the Indies and was lost off Amboina on February 15.
4. **1654** – *GOEDE HOOP*, VOC ship that was lost on July 13th south of Ambon during its voyage from Batavia to Ambon.
5. **1656** – *HARING*, Dutch East Indiaman of 100 tons (captain unknown), arrived in the Indies (Batavia) on May 3, 1644. The ship remained in the Indies as a trading ship until May 1656 when she broke up on a reef near Amboina.
6. **1672** – *WATERHOEN*, Dutch East Indiaman of 193 tons, Captain Pieter Willemsz, arrived in the Indies (Batavia) on February 14, 1665. There she remained until later wrecked at Amboina.
7. **1752** – *SCHAKENBOS*, VOC ship of 850 tons that was lost in the Manipa Strait (between Buru and Seram Islands, Moluccas) The ship was on a voyage from Batavia to Ambon.

Bali Sea
The Bali Sea lies north and northeast off the island of Bali.

8. **1653** – *DELFSHAVEN*, Dutch East Indiaman of 300 tons, Captain Kornelis van Houton, arrived in the Indies (Batavia) on October 3, 1642. Eleven years later, the ship was wrecked near Majoe (Sumbawa Island).
9. **1831** – *JOHANNA MARIA WILHELMINA*, Colonial Dutch ship, Captain R. Tower, was freighted by the government for the Moluccas and had on board about 170 troops and 130,000 guilders in specie. The ship was lost near Bali. The passengers and crew managed to reach Madura Island safely but the vessel was a total loss. The specie was saved.
10. **1857** – *JULIETTE*, schooner of unknown nationality, was on a voyage from Bali to Singapore and struck on Karangmas Reef in the Straits of Bali and was wrecked.

Banda Sea

The Banda Sea is located at latitude 6 degrees south and longitude 128 degrees east (approximate center). It lies between the islands of Buru and Seram to the north and Timor and Damar to the south.

11. **1711** – *THEEBOOM*, VOC ship of 526 tons, Captain Gilles Scharbotten, was lost at Banda.
12. **1730** – *NOORDBEEK*, VOC ship of 858 tons, Captain Herman Brand, arrived in Batavia on August 8, 1727. Three years later, the ship was lost on a voyage between Ternate (off Halmahera Island) and Bima (Sumbawa Island).
13. **1748** – *NIEUWEKERK*, VOC ship of 1,135 tons, was lost east of Binongko Island (located southeast of Sulawesi). The vessel was on route from Batavia to the Banda Islands.
14. **1766** – *GIESSENBERG*, Dutch East Indiaman of 1,150 tons, was lost just north of Buton Island (southeast Celebes). The vessel was on a voy-

age from Batavia to the Banda Islands.

Bangka and Gaspar Straits

The Bangka and Gaspar Straits are two different channels of water that are sometimes confused. The Bangka Strait lies between the islands of Sumatra and Bangka, and the Gaspar Straits lies between Bangka and Billiton islands. However, I have noticed that in many accounts of shipwrecks, Bangka Strait is named as the wreck area when the wreck was actually lost in the Gaspar Straits. In most cases, I have noted the proper strait with coordinates and/or prominent landmarks.

15. **1555** – *PORT CARAMEL*, unknown origin, struck on a rock in the Gaspar Straits and was lost while sailing from Malacca. Moors killed numerous crew members.

16. **Sometime before 1599** – *ARU*, Portuguese East Indiaman. A book of sailing directions published in Amsterdam in 1599 states that: "In the

Straits of Gaspar, also known as Straits of Clements, off the southwest coast of Billiton island, lays a small island AUR, which is so named as a result of a very rich Portuguese ship of great size being lost there with a large cargo of gold."

17. **1611** – Report of an unidentified EIC ship being lost on a reef at this spot. English survivors were massacred by the Dutch. The Dutch also recovered 18 bronze cannons from the wreck. The reef was reported to be located about eight miles south of Lepar island off the southeast tip of Bangka island.

18. **1630** – *KAMEEL*, Dutch East Indiaman of 500 tons, of the Amsterdam Chamber, was outward-bound and lost on Boomjies Eiland on February 17. This island is called Barikat Rock in today's charts.

19. **1633** – *SCHIEDAM*, VOC ship of 350 tons, of the Amsterdam Chamber, was outward-bound with a cargo of tools, ammunition and unspecified merchandise, and was lost on Boomjies Eiland in February.

20. **1638** – *DE GOEDE HOOP*, a Dutch junk, departed China for Batavia sometime between October 17, 1637 and March 18, 1838. It was laden with coarse porcelain and was lost at Lucepara Island. The porcelain was valued at 1,608 Dutch florins. (With an average value of 0.12 florins per piece, this would amount to a total of about 13,400 pieces of coarse Chinese porcelain.)

21. **1647** – *VALKENBURGE*, Dutch East Indiaman of 200 tons, of the Amsterdam Chapter (owner), which sailed from Texie, Holland on October 11, 1637 and reached Batavia on April 20, 1638. While sailing to China and Japan loaded with over 250,000 florins in coin and silver bullion, it was wrecked in June 1647 on some rocks about 25 miles off the east coast of Bangka island.

22. **1648** – *FREDERICK HENDRICK*, VOC ship of 1,100 tons and 60 bronze cannons, of the Zealand Chapter (owner), Captain Michiel Vis, which left Wielingen, Holland in 1642 was returning to Holland with a crew of 326 men and cargo valued at over 850,000 florins. On January 8, 1648, it struck a reef and sank with all its cargo and treasure and over 100 passengers and crew. This occurred near the northern end of the Bangka Strait.

23. **1670** – *DIEMEREER*, Dutch East Indiaman, 505 tons of the Amsterdam Chapter, Captain Engel Jaosz, was sailing between Batavia and Malacca on June 6, 1670 when it was wrecked on a reef near Bangka Island. This reef of rocks is located just under latitude 2 degrees south and the nearest land was 12 miles to the west.

24. **1671** – *SCHERMER*, Dutch East Indiaman of 636 tons, of the Amsterdam Chapter, Captain Hans Zwart, with 44 bronze canons and a crew of 214 men, sailing from Batavia to Holland with cargo valued at 780,000 florins, was wrecked on a voyage near Bangka on June 4, 1671 with total loss of cargo and many lives. Salvage was attempted but strong currents prevented anything from being recovered.

25. **1686** – *PRINS WILLEM HENDRICK*, Dutch East Indiaman of 1,094 tons, commanded by Captain Adriaan van Kreningen (Zeeland Chapter), was on a voyage to Siam when on September 18, 1686, it struck a reef in the Bangka Strait. After striking the reef, the ship edged off it and sank in 15 to 20 fathoms of water. Six of the crew of over 400 perished and all of the 400,000 Dutch rix dollars (coins) were totally lost. The pilot of the ship was later hung after a court martial in Batavia.

26. **1736** – An unidentified Dutch East Indiaman of approximately 500 to 700 tons, flying the flag of the Amsterdam Chapter, was seen by a passing ship, wrecked on a reef "several miles" off the northern tip of Liat island while a storm was blowing. The incident was later reported to authorities in Batavia. Rescue vessels were sent but only a few survivors were found on Liat island. The ship sank with 250,000 florins in silver aboard but neither its name nor that of its captain was given.

27. **1789** – *VANSITTART*, EIC ship of 828 tons, Captain Lestock Wilson, hit a hidden shoal (known as Vansittart's Shoal today) while surveying the Gaspar Straits. However, contrary to what some people believe, the ship did not sink there. Upon hitting the shoal, the ship started taking on much water and Captain Wilson decided to head for the nearest island to beach her and save the treasure on board. According to Captain Wilson, the *VANSITTART* ended up wrecking on a reef "three quarters of a mile from an island, the island being approximately 5 to 7 miles off the coast of Banka". This island is known as Pulo Panjang today.

    Knowing that there was no hope of re-floating the wrecked vessel, it was decided to "throw the treasure over board for later retrieval" (effectively preventing any Malay pirates from finding it too). The crew then departed in their longboats. On the first night, one of the longboats with the crew disappeared and was never seen again. Some days later, the wrecked crew met up with two other East India company ships, *ELLIOTT* and *NONSUCH*, who took them back to recover the lost treasure. However, as the *VANSITTART* settled in the sand on top of the treasure, not all of the silver chests were recovered.

    According to the book, *The Chronicles of the East India Company Trading to China, 1635–1834*, Vol. II (p. 172), "The Company had 21 ships (18,144 tons) at Canton in the season 1789; another ship, the *VANSITTART*, 828 tons, was wrecked on the coast of the island of Banka, a total loss but 33 chests of silver were salvaged from her, of which 11 were claimed for salvage." (It does not mention how many chests were lost.)

28. **1799** – A book of sailing directions published in 1799 states "that upon the rocks of FEDERICK HENDRICKS, located almost in 2 degrees of south latitude, more than 20 large ships have been lost over the years." This rock is called Karang Ular in present day maps.

Dutch VOC sailing ships at harbour.

29. **1799** – According to a book of sailing directions (published 1799), "that upon Lucepara Shoal, while sailing south for the entrance to the Straits of Bangka, a rich British East Indiaman was lost in 1765 with all of her cargo and many lives were lost". Lucipara Shoal is located at the southern entrance to the Bangka Strait.

30. **Early 1800s** – *GLASS WRECK*. This is a copper-sheathed wooden shipwreck that I dived on in December 1991. We believe it to date around the early 1800s. Its origin is unknown but the Southeast Asia Salvage Company recovered two English iron cannons from it (a four- and a six-pounder), many different types of bottles and also some porcelain. The ship was laying upright, virtually intact and was full of cargo. As it was monsoon season and the weather was rough, we were only able to dive on it for two days and were forced to return to Singapore. We never returned to dive on this wreck again. This wreck is located about 32 miles northeast of the Sungai Baturusi (Baturusi River) mouth entrance on the central east coast of Bangka Island. (see Chapter 4)

31. **1806** – *FORBES*, English country trading ship which sank on November 11th at the south end of the Gaspar Straits during its voyage from China to India. It is rumoured that the vessel had a cargo of gold and porcelain on board.

32. **1816** – Discovery Rock (a cliff), so named after a British survey ship by that name which surveyed the area in 1813. Three years later in 1816, a rich Portuguese ship from Macau was lost upon this rock. The rock is located between Lapar and Liat islands off the southeast tip of Bangka Island.

33. **1816** – *AMELIA*, Portuguese ship, was wrecked on Alceste Cliff. It is reported that many other ships have wrecked on this reef. On today's charts it is known as Karang Alceste and is located on the northwest side of Liat Island.

34. **1817** – *ALCESTE*, HMS (English ship) was on a voyage to China with a famous ambassador on board. The ship was wrecked on this reef which now bears its name, Alceste Cliff. The wreck was stranded and later looted by pirates.

35. **1817** – *LE MINERVE*, French ship of 805 tons, was reported missing this year in the Gaspar Straits (This ship was salvaged by a French company, Matcosub, in 1991).

36. **1824** – In a book of sailing directions written in 1847, it was reported: "Severn Bank (Shoal), The ship *SEVERN* from New York struck this bank and got off after heaving 30 tons of ballast overboard. The *COLUMBIAN* from New York was lost on this bank in March 1824 on her return voyage from China (Canton)."

37. **1845** – Sunken English vessel (name unknown), the mast heads of which were still seen above water at Lucipara Island. The vessel lay sunk in six-and-a-half fathoms of water with its bow in an east-south-east direction while between the masts only four-and-a-half fathoms were sounded.

38. **1845** – *COLUMBIAN*, (origin unspecified), on April 7 this ship, which was bound from Sydney to Singapore, struck on a reef that is known as Karang Severn today, anchored nearby and sank soon afterwards.

39. **1845** – *GONDOLIER*, English ship, was lost on Warren Hastings Reef. Later the ship was observed to be in a south 22 degrees west direction from the reef.

40. **1847** – A book of sailing instructions written in 1847 states: "a ship from New York was lost upon this reef and likewise a China junk not long afterwards". On today's charts, this bank is known as Karang Belvedere.

41. **Year unknown** – In a book of sailing directions written in 1847, it states: "Linga Island – the *STIRLING CASTLE* was wrecked on a shoal that projects from the Third Point, counting westward from the east point of the island."

42. **1850** – *CORNELIUS HAJA*, Dutch schooner, was wrecked on Barikat Rock in April 1850 while carrying 50 tons of tin ingots and other products.

43. **1851** – *MEMNON*, American clipper ship, was lost in the Gaspar Straits a few days out from Whampoa (China).

44. **1853** – *BERENICE*, British merchant vessel, caught fire and burnt while sailing through the Gaspar Straits. It was not known whether any of the ship's crew survived.

45. **1854** – *HENDRIK WESTER*, Dutch ship, was on a voyage from Whampoa (China) bound to Bremen and wrecked on Alceste Reef in the Gaspar

SHIPWRECKS AND SUNKEN TREASURE IN SOUTHEAST ASIA

Straits. Much of the cargo was saved by the crew.

46. **1854** – On June 17 in this year, the masts of a sunken wreck (name unknown) were spotted in 13 to 14 fathoms of water. Two Brothers Islands thence bearing northwest by north 1/2 degrees north, the North Watcher island southwest by west 1/2 degrees west.

47. **1857** – *TRANSIT*, British HMS steamer ship, Captain Chambers, after leaving Corunna, struck on a coral reef in the Bangka Strait at 9 a.m. on July 10. About an hour and a half afterwards, the vessel went down. Her stern ended up in 11 fathoms water and her bow appearing above the surface. The troops (part of the 90th regiment), and crew, were safely landed on the island of Bangka but little or nothing was saved from the wrecked vessel.

48. **1857** – *BRITAIN'S QUEEN*, London barque, Captain Morris, departed Singapore on July 29 for Falmouth with a general cargo, struck on the east side of the north end of Lucipara Shoal in the Bangka Straits about midnight on August 7. Every exertion was made by the crew to get the vessel off the reef, but they proved fruitless. By August 11, the vessel was nearly full of water and her back broken. Crew abandoned the wreck and arrived back in Singapore on August 16, via the Dutch barque, *HINGOAN*.

49. **1858** – *VESTA*, English ship, Captain R. Potter, which was bound for Singapore, had encountered very bad weather and foundered in the Gaspar Straits in December. Crew reached Pamanukan (Java) on January 11, 1859.

50. **1860** – *INTERPID*, American ship, Captain Gardner, from China to New York, was wrecked on a reef in the Gaspar Straits on March 31. The ship was looted by Malay pirates before some of the cargo could be salvaged by the steamer *SHANDON*, commanded by Captain Anderson. The *SHANDON* saved a number of porcelain vases and other objects, but it was found that what remained of the silk and crape goods was completely damaged. There was a large quantity of Chinese fireworks on board and gunpowder from these had mixed with the water in the hold, damaging the rest of the goods and rendering it impossible for divers to go down. In another account, the *INTERPID* was reported as lost on Belvidere Reef in 1860.

51. **1862** – *SALACIA*, London barque, Captain Howe, departed Singapore on May 10 bound for London with a general cargo, and struck on an unknown reef on May 23rd at 8 a.m. and was obliged to be abandoned. The reef she struck is described as being in about latitude 1 degrees, 10 minutes south and longitude 106 degrees, 32 minutes east, Gaspar Island bearing about south-south-east, 80 miles distance. The captain and some of the crew managed to reach Singapore in the ship's boats on May 27.

52. **1863** – *CHARLES HENRY*, Belgian brig from Antwerp, bound for Manilla, struck on the Arang Marai reef near Pulo Lapar on July 22, and

afterwards became a total wreck. The cargo was machinery and general goods.

53. **1864** – ISLE O'MAY, London barque of 393 tons, Captain Gray, struck on the Arang Marai reef near Pulo Lapar on June 13. There were hopes to get the barque off the reef but it is unclear whether the vessel was re-floated.

54. **1868** – ANDREW JACKSON, American ship, while sailing from Shanghai bound for America, ran on a reef in the Gaspar Straits on December 4.

55. **1870** – SAMUEL RUSSEL, American ship, wrecked in Gaspar Straits, November 23.

56. **1872** – MARIE THERESE, a three-masted single deck French barque of 503 tons, departed from Bordeaux (France) on September 30, 1871. The barque was bound for Saigon with a cargo of fine French wine and champagne. On February 29, the vessel struck on Cooper Reef in the Gaspar Straits and shortly thereafter sank. This ship was salvaged by a French company, Matcosub, in 1991. (See also Chapter 4)

57. **1878** – WILLEM KRONPRINS, Dutch steamship that collided on November 9th with the ATJEH in the Bangka Strait and sank soon afterwards in 13 fathoms of water. Salvage was attempted at the time of loss but the results are unknown.

Carimata Strait

The Carimata Strait is located at latitude 3 degrees south, longitude 109 degrees east (approximate center). It lies between the island of Billiton and Borneo.

58. **1797** – ONTARIO, American ship, Captain J. Whetton, was on a voyage from China and wrecked on an uncharted shoal in the Carimata Straits on January 4. This shoal is known on todays charts as Ontario Shoal. The ship was said to have been carrying a load on fine Chinese porcelain and other goods from the Far East. (In 1992, a salvage group claimed to had located this ship but I don't know whether it was salvaged or not.)

59. **After 1797** – COROMANDEL, English ship, was wrecked on the Ontario Shoal, sometime after the ONTARIO was wrecked there.

Celebes Islands

Today the largest island of this group is known as Sulawesi, and its approximate center is at latitude 2 degrees south, longitude 121 degrees east. There are many other smaller islands in the group.

60. **1650** – AAGTEKERK, Dutch East Indiaman of 100 tons (captain unknown), arrived in the Indies (Batavia) on November 4, 1644. There the ship remained until it was wrecked on a reef near the Celebes on

March 4, 1650.

61. **1650** – *BERGEN OP ZOOM*, VOC ship of 300 tons, Captain David Dingemans, arrived in the Indies (Batavia) on August 17, 1641. There the ship remained until it was wrecked on a reef south of the Celebes on March 4.

62. **1650** – *LUIPAARD*, Dutch East Indiaman of 320 tons (captain unknown), arrived in the Indies (Batavia) on August 30, 1642. The vessel was wrecked on a reef south of the Celebes on March 4.

63. **1650** – *JUFFER*, Dutch East Indiaman of 480 tons (captain unknown), arrived in the Indies (Batavia) on July 9, 1645. There the vessel remained until its career ended when it was wrecked on a reef south of the Celebes on March 4.

64. **1660** – Portuguese East Indiaman, under the command of Francisco Viera De Figueiredo, was lost at Ujung Pandang harbour (southwest Celebes) on March 29th. The ship was departing Ujung Pandang harbour for Goa (India). Rumour has it that the vessel had gold on board.

65. **1660** – On June 8th, two ships were lost in a sea battle against the Dutch (one ship was Portuguese and the other was of unknown origin). This battle took place at Ujung Pandang harbour (southwestern Celebes). Some gold and silver were supposedly lost with these ships.

66. **1663** – *WALVIS*, Dutch East Indiaman of 1,000 tons, Captain Albert Bruinvis, arrived in the Indies (Batavia) on July 12, 1660. Three years later on January 7, the ship was wrecked on a reef at Salayar.

67. **1685** – *AARDENBURG*, Dutch East Indiaman of 482 tons (captain unknown), sank near Buton in August.

Flores Sea

The approximate center of the Flores Sea is at latitude 7 degrees 30 minutes south, longitude 121 degrees east, between the islands of Sulawesi to the north and Flores to the south.

68. **1580** – Portuguese nao (name unknown), commanded by Mathias de Albuquerque (descendent of Alfonso), was on a voyage from Malacca to Amboina (where he was to become the naval commander). On the way, he was shipwrecked near Solor where he remained for four months.

69. **1642** – *MAAN*, Dutch East Indiaman of 200 tons (captain unknown), arrived in the Indies (Batavia) on September 19, 1638. The ship remained in the Indies and four years later, on April 10, ran ashore at Solor Island.

70. **1650** – *TIJER*, VOC ship of 1,000 tons, was lost on a reef south of the Celebes on March 4th. The vessel was on route from Batavia to Ambon (Moluccas).

71. **1748** – *MAARSSEVEEN*, Dutch East Indiaman of 850 tons, blew up and sank just east of Salayar Island (Celebes) while on a voyage from the Banda Islands to Batavia (Java). Rumour has it that there may have been some gold on board.

72. **1796** – *OCEAN*, EIC ship of 1,189 tons, Captain Andrew Patton, in the company of several other East Indiamen passed northward through the Allass (Alas) Strait on January 31 at 4 p.m. With the rain and severe squalls, the fleet unfortunately mistook the Schiedam Islands for the Postillions. Upon realizing their mistake, they immediately turned sharply, but some of the ships perceiving breakers ahead, turned again, set courses and continued working until daylight. The EIC vessels *ALFRED* and *WOODFORD* struck on a reef off Kalatoa (Kalaotoa) Island but fortunately backed off.

The *OCEAN* was driven by the strong current onto the reef and wrecked before daylight. The other ships did not witness this incident and carried on sailing. The shipwrecked crew managed to carry a few necessities ashore from the wreck. For 14 days, the local islanders promised to take them to Amboina Island in their *proas* (wooden fishing boats). However, they were stalling because they had other treacherous plans for Captain Patton and crew. The captain soon realized this and decided to attack first. During this fight, both sides lost several men and many were wounded.

Fortunately, a Macassar man was on the island at the time and agreed to take the shipwrecked sailors to Amboina. They left this inhospitable island on February 19 and arrived at Amboina on February 28.

In an alternative account, the *OCEAN* was reported wrecked on the island of Kalao after the engagement with a French squadron of six frigates on January 8, 1797. The *OCEAN* was in company with a fleet of EIC China ships when they were surprised off the extremity of Java by the French fleet. The Indiamen were carrying valuable cargoes of specie and merchandise. The *OCEAN* was wrecked on the island of Kalao Tua four days after the engagement with the French fleet.

73. **1802** – *BANGALORE*, a ship which was bound from Amboina towards the Allass Strait, struck upon a hidden shoal while sailing through the Flores Sea on April 12 at 9 p.m. The anchor was dropped but because of the steepness of the coral bank, the attempt to anchor was unsuccessful. The vessel sank completely soon after.

74. **1863** – *FRANKFURT OLD*, British barque of Liverpool, Captain Hicks, left Cardiff on October 29, 1862 bound for Shanghai with a cargo of coal. On February 19 at 7:45 p.m., the vessel was proceeding with a stiff breeze when she struck on the coral reef Lambuang near Kalatua and Bonerate Islands (southeast of Salayar Island) and immediately sank. The crew consisted of 23 persons. Of these, there was only one

survivor – the boatswain. He survived by floating on the ship's wreckage for four days and five nights without food or water. Upon seeing some natives in a *sampan* (rowing boat), he shouted and was picked up by them and was brought to a nearby island. There he remained for a month ill with delirium and a fever. He later found out that he was on the island of Kalatua. The boatswain had no idea as to the fate of the other 22 crew members. Besides the cargo of coal, there was said to have been about £50,000 in gold and silver specie on board.

Halmahera Sea
The Halmahera Sea lies between the islands of Halmahera (to the west) and New Guinea (to the east).

75. **1607** – *ENKHUIZEN*, VOC ship of 300 tons, Captain Klaas Thijsz Collet, arrived at Bantam (west Java) on August 21, 1605. Two years later, the vessel ran aground off Halmahera Island.

Java Sea
The approximate center of the Java Sea is at latitude 5 degrees south, longitude 115 degrees east. The island of Borneo is to the north and Java is to the south.

76. **1601** – On December 26, there was a sea battle off Bantam (west Java) between a Dutch and Portuguese fleet. The Dutch fleet consisted of four galleons and one galley, which were *GUELDERLAND* (520 tons), *SEALAND* (400 tons), *UTRECHT* (240 tons), *WATCHER* (120 tons) and the *DOVE* (50 tons). The Portuguese fleet consisted of 8 big galleons and 22 galleys (names unknown). The ferocious battle lasted for six or seven days. Two of the Portuguese galleons and three of their galleys were so badly battered and bruised that the crew themselves set the ships on fire to try and take down some of the Dutch vessels as a last ditch effort. Fortunately for the Dutch, they were able to elude them. None of the Dutch vessels were lost during this encounter.

77. **1601** – PIE vessel, under the command of Pereira De Sande, was on route from Malacca to Ambon and was lost on the Rocks of Peressada in northeast Java. The ship supposedly had a cargo of gold and silver specie.

78. **1611 or 1613** – *TRADES INCREASE*, EIC ship of 1,293 tons, was at Bantam harbour where its sheathing was being seen to. However, even before one side of the vessel was completed, the ship fell over on its side and became a total loss. This tragedy caused the death of many of the ship's crew and Javanese workers. The ship was afterwards set on fire by angry Javanese, where it burned to the waterline and sank to its watery grave.

Close up of dolphins on a Dutch cannon recovered off Port Dickson near Malacca in 1993.

‡ **1613** – *TRADES INCREASE*, EIC ship of 1,100 tons, under the command of Sir Henry Middleton, sailed from Europe for the east on April 1st, 1610. While proceeding into Bantam, the vessel ran upon a rock and sprang a leak. While being repaired, the ship careened over and was afterwards set on fire and totally destroyed by the Javanese.

79. **1617** – *HECTOR*, EIC ship, Captain William Edwardes, was lost off Jakarta (Batavia) in June.

80. **1618** – *BLACK LION*, English East Indiaman (tonnage unknown), was at anchor off Jakarta (Batavia), when at midnight on December 25, the ship was set on fire due to the carelessness of the crew and was burnt down to the water's edge. All of the crew managed to get onto another nearby anchored EIC vessel.

81. **1623** – *REFUGE*, EIC ship, was lost off Semarang (east Java) while on route from England to Asia.

82. **1627** – *BANTAM*, VOC ship of 800 tons, caught fire on March 24th and burned while at the Batavia quay wall. Cargo was most probably salvaged shortly afterwards.

83. **1632** – *NIJMEGEN*, Dutch East Indiaman, was lost near Batavia shortly after departing for its homeward-bound voyage in August. The ship was supposed to have some Asian porcelain on board.

84. **1633** – *BREEDAM*, VOC ship of 200 tons, Captain Michiel Vis, arrived in the Indies (Batavia) on May 24, 1633. The ship stayed in the Indies and was eventually wrecked near the Duizend Islands (Thousand Islands, north of Batavia).

85. **1633** – *DELFSHAVEN*, Dutch East Indiaman of 400 tons, (captain unknown), the vessel arrived in the Indies (Batavia) on September 8, 1632. The following year in Batavia on November 12, the vessel exploded because of carelessness.

86. **1653** – *ZEEMEEUW*, Dutch East Indiaman of 100 tons, Captain Alexander Hendriksz, was lost east of Batavia.

87. **1657** – *LILLO*, Dutch East Indiamen of 240 tons, Captain Jean Lalphart, was bound for Batavia (via Pernambuco, Sulawesi) and was wrecked on the roadstead (harbour entrance) of Batavia.

88. **1658** – *WINDHOND*, VOC ship of 360 tons, was lost on Boompjes Island (northeast of Batavia, Java) while on a local trading voyage.

89. **1663** – *GRIFFIOEN*, Dutch East Indiaman of 560 tons (captain unknown), arrived in the Indies (Batavia) on October 28, 1647 and was used at Onrust (out of Batavia). The ship sank on November 16.

90. **1670** – *NIEUWENDAM*, Dutch East Indiaman of 210 tons (captain unknown), arrived in the Indies (Batavia) on June 18, 1663. The ship stayed in the Indies and was wrecked between Bima and Macassar on the night of October 1, 1670.

91. **1673** – *STOMPNEUS*, VOC ship, Captain Antony Van Doorn, was sunk at Japara (Samarang Bay) by the EIC ship *ZANTE*. In the attack on the *ZANTE*, Dutch records state that the *STOMPNEUS* was sunk owing to the "cowardice and incompetence" of her captain, Antony van Doorn.

92. **1684** – *HUIS TE KLEEF*, Dutch East Indiaman of 564 tons, Captain Gerrit Albertsz Schellinger, arrived in the Indies (Batavia) on August 16, 1675. During a voyage north to Palembang (Sumatra) the ship was wrecked on a reef near the Thousand Islands on September 1.

93. **1684** – *BODE*, Dutch East Indiamen of 96 tons, Captain Adriaan Roelofsz van Asperen, arrived in the Indies (Batavia) on November 18, 1674. On September 13, the ship was wrecked on a reef near the Thousand Islands.

94. **1686** – *KROONVOGEL*, Dutch East Indiaman of 108 tons, Captain Lucas Genzenwinner, arrived in the Indies (Batavia) on July 4, 1676. On February 11, 1686, the ship ran ashore and was wrecked at Alkmaar Island near Batavia.

95. **1690** – *ZIJPE*, Dutch East Indiaman of 488 tons, Captain Jan Modderman, arrived in the Indies (Batavia) on May 12, 1674. The ship was later blown up at the roadstead of Batavia.

96. **1697** – *BRONSTEDE*, Dutch East Indiaman of 253 tons, Captain Jakob Barendsz Sonbeek, arrived in the Indies (Batavia) on October 10, 1686. Eleven years later on August 21, the ship was wrecked on the roads of Semarang (east of Batavia) because of leakage.

97. **1698** – *HONSELAARSDIJK*, Dutch East Indiaman of 722 tons, Captain Kornelis Ole, arrived in the Indies (Batavia) on February 28, 1691. Seven years later, the ship was wrecked at the roads of Batavia.

98. **1702** – *SCHELLAG*, VOC ship of 290 tons, Captain Jakob de la Palma,

arrived in the Indies (Batavia) on September 10, 1700. On the night of November 21, the ship sank on the roads of Batavia.

99. **1719** – *OEGSTGEEST*, VOC ship of 576 tons, Captain Pieter Jansz Bruin, was lost at Grisee (village located north of Surabaya) during this year.

100. **1728** – *OUWERKERK*, VOC ship of 658 tons, Captain Jan de Vos, was wrecked near Japara (north of Semarang) during this year.

101. **1740** – *VALKENISSE*, Dutch East Indiaman of 1,150 tons, Captain Elias Moeninx, arrived in the Indies (Batavia) on January 21, 1734. Six years later during the month of September, the ship was wrecked at Bantam (west of Batavia).

102. **1744** – *KASTEEL VAN WOERDEN*, Dutch East Indiaman of 850 tons, was lost after striking a rock 14 kilometers (9 miles) from Pamanukan (east of Batavia, Java).

103. **1746** – *HOFWEGEN*, Dutch East Indiaman of 650 tons, Captain Jan de Wit, arrived in the Indies (Batavia) on October 7, 1742. Four years later, on September 1, the ship exploded at the roads of Batavia.

104. **1765** – *PIJLSWAART*, Dutch East Indiaman of 880 tons, was lost at the roads to Batavia on February 24th. The ship was on route from the Netherlands.

105. **1784** – *EUROPA*, VOC ship of 1,200 tons, struck on the Rock of Indramajoe (a few kilometers east of Batavia) and sank. The vessel was on an inter-Asian trading excursion at the time.

106. **1789** – *JONGE FRANK*, Dutch East Indiaman of 592 tons, Captain Jacob Veer, while at the Cape of Good Hope, took over part of the cargo of the homeward-bound vessel *MARIA*, wrecked there in August 1788. The *JONGE FRANK* then proceeded to Batavia, arriving on December 24, 1789. At the roads of Batavia, the ship sank. The cargo of the *MARIA* was valued at 254,877 florins.

107. **1794** – *INDUS*, Dutch East Indiaman of 1,150 tons, Captain Matthijs Laurens Koster, arrived in the Indies (Batavia) on May 20, 1791. Three years later, the *INDUS* was burnt down in the roads of Batavia.

108. **1795 or 1796** – *HERTOG VAN BRUNSWIJK*, Dutch East Indiaman of 1,150 tons, Captain Jan Olhof, arrived in the Indies (Batavia) on July 9, 1794. In the year 1795 or 1796, the vessel was wrecked off Batavia.

109. **1796** – *DRAAK*, VOC ship of 1,150 tons, Captain Anthonie van Rijn, first arrived in the Indies (Batavia) on July 13, 1793. Three years later, while being at anchor in the roads of Batavia, the *DRAAK* was struck by lightning and burnt down.

110. **1817** – *WENA*, Dutch ship, was wrecked near Batavia while on a voyage from Rotterdam (Netherlands) to Batavia. Some of the cargo was salvaged at the time of loss.

111. **1854** – *ZINGARI*, American barque, bound from Batavia to Singapore was lost on Brouwers Shoal in June this year. The captain, crew and passengers were saved.

112. **1856** – *ROBERTUS HENDRIKUS*, Dutch ship, lying in the roads of Batavia,

was discovered to be on fire on the morning of June 10. Every effort was made by the officers and crew to get the fire under control but without effect. The fire quickly spread and by noon, the ship had sunk, leaving only the bowspeit above water. The vessel was bound for Samarang and had on board £80,000 sterling in specie belonging to the government, 1,000 picals of tin, 1,500 picals of coffee and quantity of coals and gunny bags. It is not mentioned if any of this lost cargo was salvaged or not.

113. **1856** – *CHINA*, English merchant vessel, Captain Ayers, was on a voyage from Manilla to London and on the night of June 29, struck on a reef near the Thousand Islands. The vessel was got off the reef but very soon afterwards sank. The captain and crew of 27 were obliged to take to their boats and were picked up the following day by the American vessel, *CYNTHIA*, under the command of Captain Barblet. They arrived safely in Batavia on July 1. The *CHINA* had on board a cargo of sugar.

114. **1857** – *LIEUTENANT ADMIRAL STELLI NGWERF*, Dutch schooner, was lost at latitude 7 degrees 1 minutes south, longitude 110 degrees 27 minutes east (central Java) during its voyage from Semarang (Java) to Singapore. The ship supposedly had specie to the value of US$20,000 to $30,000 on board.

115. **1858** – *NICHOLAS CEZARD*, French ship, hit a reef in the Java Sea and sank.

116. **1860** – *DERKINA TITIA*, Dutch ship, Captain Evink, bound from Macau to Java, was totally lost on Arends Island on September 17. The crew reached Surabaya in safety.

117. **1861** – *AGATHA MARIA*, Dutch sailing ship that was lost on June 17th on a reef near Cilacap (central southern Java) at approximately latitude 7 degrees 41 minutes south, longitude 109 degrees 05 minutes east. The vessel was on route from Cilacap (Java) to Amsterdam (Netherlands). There was a salvage attempt at the time of loss but results are unknown.

118. **1862** – *PIONEER*, American ship, bound from Manilla (Philippines) to Liverpool (England) was lost on the island Karimon Java on December 27. The crew re-conveyed at Samarang.

119. **1862 or early 1863** – *SPEED*, Siamese junk sailing under English colors, bound from Batavia to Bangkok, struck on the island Karimon Java and sank. The crew re-conveyed at Samarang.

120. **1875** – *NEVA*, a French Messageries Maritime vessel, was lost 13 kilometers (eight miles) from Batavia on August 7th. The ship was on route from Singapore to Batavia (Java).

Madura
The island's latitude is 7 degrees south and longitude is 113 degrees 20 minutes east. It is located just off the northwest coast of Java.

121. **1677** – *DAMIATE*, VOC ship of 750 tons, Captain Arend Simonsz Vader, arrived in the Indies (Batavia) on June 10, 1671. Six years later, on August 31, the ship ran ashore east of Madura Island. Eighteen men were drowned.

122. **1677** – *PAGADET*, Dutch East Indiaman of 90 tons (captain unknown), arrived in the Indies (Batavia) on December 19, 1671. Six years later, on August 31, the ship ran ashore east of Madura Island. Eighteen men were drowned.

123. **1854** – *ARTEMISIA*, British ship of London, Captain Banes, was on a voyage from Auckland (New Zealand) bound to Singapore, when the ship was lost on the night of July 27 on the Karang Taket Reef off Kangean. The crew consisted of 32 people including the captain's wife. They all arrived safely in Surabaya by long boat on July 30.

124. **1858** – *SOUBURG*, Dutch ship, was on a voyage from Surabaya to China and struck a reef in the Madura Strait and immediately foundered.

Makassar Strait

The Makassar Strait is located at latitude 1 degrees 30 minutes south, longitude 118 degrees east (approximate center). The island of Borneo is to the west and Sulawesi is to the east.

125. **1617** – *THOMASINE*, EIC ship of 133 tons, struck on a shoal and sank near Macassar in September this year. The ship was on its homeward voyage from the Moluccas laden with nutmegs and mace. Most of her goods and men were saved.

126. **1618** – *THOMAS*, EIC ship that was lost in the Strait of Desalon, 106 kilometers (66 miles) off Ujung Pandang, Celebes. Some of the cargo was salvaged at the time of loss.

127. **1664** – *LEEUWIN*, Dutch East Indiaman of 400 tons (captain unknown), the vessel arrived in the Indies (Batavia) on September 27, 1655. Nine years later on December 24, the vessel was wrecked near Macassar.

128. **1668** – *GEIT*, VOC ship of 160 tons (captain unknown), arrived in the Indies (Batavia) on July 14, 1668. The following month on August 4, the ship was wrecked near Macassar.

129. **1668** – *ZIERIKZEE*, Dutch East Indiaman of 400 tons, Captain Jut Jokobsz Buis, first arrived in the Indies (Batavia) on July 2, 1660. Eight years later, the ship sank off Macassar.

130. **1700** – *VOETBOOG*, Dutch East Indiaman of 595 tons, Captain Adriaan de Ruiter, departed Batavia on January 21 for a homeward-bound voyage to the Netherlands and was wrecked off Pernambuco (Sulawesi) on May 29. The cargo was valued at 233,251 florins.

131. **1761** – *KLEVERSKERKE*, VOC ship of 850 tons, was lost between southeast Borneo and southwest Sulawesi while on a voyage from Batavia to Ujung Pandang (Celebes).

132. **1855** – *SYED KHAN*, schooner, capsized in a heavy squall and sank in the Strait of Makassar off Cape Mandhar.

133. **1858** – *MACASSAR*, Belgian ship, Captain Brarens, was on a voyage and encountered bad weather. This caused the ship to wreck on the Brilbank at 2 a.m. on December 27. The ship being severely damaged and full of water, the captain and 25 crew members took the ship's boats and proceeded to Boelecomba.

134. **1863** – *CELEBES*, HNM steamship, was wrecked on a reef opposite Passier, supposed to be Hercules reef, on July 15. The crew were taken off the wreck site by HNM's steamers, *ADMIRAL DE RUYTER* and *DE VECHE*, and brought to Macassar.

Moluccas

The main island of this group now known as Halmahera, with its approximate center at latitude 1 degrees north, longitude 128 degrees east.

135. **1512** – Portuguese East Indiaman under the command of Francisco Serrao which was lost on the Isle of Luco Pino, south of Ambon, Moluccas. The ship was originally routed from Malacca to Moluccas. It supposedly had specie on board.

136. **1527** – Spanish nau (name unknown), under the command of D. Martim Inheques, was lost in Febuary at Tidore harbour (island just south of Ternate). The nau was loaded with cargo and artillery. This was one of Magellan's ships.

137. **1571** – Portuguese East Indiaman, under the command of Sancho De Vasconcelos, lost at Cape Nousanive 58 kilometers (36 miles) from Tidore, Halmahera. The ship was on a voyage from Goa (India) to Ambon (Moluccas). Specie was rumoured to have been lost with the vessel.

138. **1601** – *HENDRIK FREDERIK*, Dutch East Indiamen of 350 tons, was lost in February or March at Ternate, Halmahera during its voyage from the Netherlands to Ternate. Specie was reported to have been lost with the vessel.

139. **1625** – *GRIFFION*, Dutch East Indiaman of 320 tons, Captain Pieter Kornelisz Hartloop, arrived in the Indies (Batavia) on August 29, 1625. The ship remained in the Indies under the commission of the VOC but was lost near the Moluccas that year.

Riau Archipelago

This group consists of many islands, Bintan being the largest. The group's approximate center is at latitude 1 degrees 20 minutes north, longitude 104 degrees east.

140. **1641** – *UTRECHT*, VOC ship of 350 tons, Captain Kornelis Simonsz van der Veer, was sent to and remained in the Indies and in May 1641, the

vessel ran ashore in the Strait of Doerian (Durian Strait?) and was wrecked.

141. **1751** – *GELDERMALSEN*, Dutch East Indiaman of 1,150 tons, Captain Morel, departed China on November 30 for a homeward voyage to the Netherlands, was wrecked between China and the Cape of Good Hope. Thirty-two members of the crew were saved. The ship's cargo was valued at 714,936 florins. This ship was salvaged by Captain Michael Hatcher in 1985 and 140,000 pieces of porcelain along with 125 gold bars were recovered. (See Chapter 3)

142. **1845** – *PARSEE*, British barque of 390 tons, was wrecked northeast of Bintan Island in November. Some cargo salvaged at the time of loss.

Old map of the islands making up the Riau Archipelago.

143. **1846** – *FREDERICK VI*, P&O Line British mail ship, sank on July 6th at latitude 0 degrees 36 minutes south, longitude 105 degrees 17 minutes east.

144. **1856** – *MERCURIUS*, Dutch barque, was lost on the north coast of Bintan island. The ship had on board 250 Chinese passengers.

145. **1862** – *SUSANNAH*, Hamburg barque, Captain Russ, was bound for Falmouth and was lost at Bintang Point on February 19. She had on board the crew of the wrecked Hamburg vessel, *MALACCA*, which was lost on Pratas Shoal, South China Sea. Both crews were brought safely to Singapore.

Sumatra

This is one of the larger islands of the Indonesian archipelago. The latitude lies between 5 degrees north 40 minutes and 6 degrees south. Longitude runs from 95 degrees to 106 degrees east.

146. **1508** – *SANTA CLARA*, Portuguese carrack, was lost off Polveira Island (east coast of Sumatra), in the Straits of Malacca. Vessel was said to have had silver on board.

147. **1511** – *FLOR DO MAR*, Portuguese nao of 400 to 700 tons, under the command of Admiral Alfonso de Albuquerque, was on a voyage from Malacca back to Lisbon with what Albuquerque himself said was "The richest treasure on earth that I have ever seen". It was all of

the spoils of Malacca which had been sacked and pillaged by the Portuguese. This rich treasure included more than 60 tons of gold booty of all different shapes and sizes, including guilded furniture and the Malaccan sultan's throne. Ingots and coinage valued at over 15,000,000 crowns came from the sultan's palace alone. An equal amount of gold was also pillaged from the rich merchants of Malacca, most of whom were either murdered or had fled the city. More than 200 chests of diamonds, emeralds, rubies, sapphires, and other precious stones were also included in spoils. However, this fabulous treasure never made it to Portugal.

Against the advice of his pilots who felt that December was too late in the year to make a safe voyage back to Lisbon, Albuquerque loaded the treasures on the "old and unseaworthy" FLOR DO MAR, and three other vessels: the TRINIDAD, the ENXOBREGAS and an unnamed junk. A few days after leaving Malacca, they encountered a fierce storm. The ENXOBREGAS and the junk went to the bottom with all their crew. (Other accounts say that the junk was seized mutineers who then sailed off and were never heard off again.) The FLOR DO MAR soon afterwards struck a reef just after rounding the northeastern-most tip of Sumatra. The crew of the remaining ship, TRINIDAD, witnessed this and dropped anchor nearby. Due to the severity of the storm, they dared not risk venturing too near the wrecked FLOR. Albuquerque had his men make up a small raft, with which he and five officers made passage with great difficulty to the nearby waiting TRINIDAD.

Upon leaving the FLOR, Albuquerque vowed to return with assistance for its wrecked crew but he did just the opposite. Albuquerque ordered the TRINIDAD's crew to cut the anchor and set sail for India. The FLOR DO MAR afterwards broke up on the reef. Of the 400 people, only three survivors managed to swim to the Sumatran coast.

148. **1516** – Portuguese East Indiaman (name unknown), under the command of Giovanni da Empoli. The vessel caught fire while being loaded with pepper off Pase (Pasai) and sank with the cargo.

149. **1516** – Portuguese ship, under the command of Antonio Pacheco, was lost NE of Sumatra at approximate latitude 5 degrees 20 minutes north, longitude 97 degrees east. The vessel was on route from India to China.

150. **1527** – *MECA NAU*, a Muslim Achinese ship, called by this name by the Portuguese. The nau was loaded with cargo when it sank in Febuary in the Achem estuary (north Sumatra, present day Banda Aceh).

151. **1527** – Portuguese ship, under the command of Francisco de Melo, was lost near Aceh, north Sumatra while on a voyage from Aceh to Goa (India).

152. **1561** – *SAO PAULO*, Portuguese East Indiaman (tonnage and captain

unknown), departed from Lisbon in April 1560 with about 450 passengers and $500,000 in silver, gold and jewels. She was bound for the Indian continent but due to the incompetence of the navigator, they completely missed it. On January 22, 1561, the ship ended up wrecking on the west coast of Sumatra, near the village of Sysak. Most of the valuables were taken off the ship before she broke up, but in the confusion, some of her treasures may have been left behind.

153. **1565** – Achinese ship, burnt and sank during a sea battle with the Portuguese in March off north Sumatra. It was on a voyage from Iran to Aceh (north Sumatra). The ship was rumoured to have had a cargo of silver, gold and jewels on board.

154. **1565** – *SAN SEBASTIAO*, Portuguese galleon, burnt and sank in March off north Sumatra while engaged in a battle against the Achinese.

155. **1588** – Portuguese carrack, under the command of Leonardo Da Sa, was lost off Aceh (north Sumatra) while on route from Goa to China.

156. **1616** – *AEOLUS KLINE*, VOC ship of 240 tons, was lost on August 25th after striking the Rocks of Enggano (located off of Enggano Island, southwest Sumatra) while voyaging from Coromandel (India) to Bantam (west Java). Very little cargo was salvaged at the time of loss.

‡ **1616** – *KLINE ADOLUS*, VOC ship of 240 tons, Captain Pieter Kornelisz, while sailing from Coromandel (India) to Bantam (Java), the ship foundered on the rocks off Engano Island on August 25.

‡ **1616** – *FLEINE AEOLUS*, Dutch East Indiaman of 240 tons, Captain Pieter Kornelisz, floundered on the rocks of Engano Island on August 25, 1616.

157. **1618** – *SUN*, English East Indiaman of 700 tons, was on a voyage from England bound for Bantam (Java) travelling in company with four other East Indiamen (*MOON*, *CLOVE*, *SAMSON* and *PEPPERCORN*), and in late November, was wrecked upon the Ile of Engano. Apparently, this incident happened at night and the four Indiamen in her company did not witness the disappearance of the vessel. On November 28, two boats with survivors from the *SUN* arrived at Bantam. They brought news of the lost ship along with many of her men. On December 3, the EIC ship *BEE* set sail for Engano, according to her crew, "in hopes to recover some money and goods" that went down with the *SUN*. Being beaten back by foul weather and unable to get out of the Straits of Sunda, the *BEE* returned to Bantam from an unsuccessful salvage attempt on December 14. On December 16, the English East Indiamen flotilla got word that a Dutch fleet had arrived at Jakarta and proceeded there to engage in battle. There is no further mention as to any attempts to return to the *SUN* to salvage her lost goods.

158. **1619** – *HOORN*, VOC ship of 700 tons, sank on December 14th approximately 130 km (80 miles) west of Sumatra at latitude 5 degrees south. The ship was routed from the Netherlands to Bantam.

159. **1619** – *ZEELANDIA*, VOC ship of 800 tons, Captain Jan van Meldert, arrived in the Indies on October 16, 1619. There the ship remained and was wrecked sometime during that year on the west coast of Sumatra.

160. **1630** – *WALCHERN*, Dutch East Indiaman of 500 to 600 tons (captain unknown), arrived in the Indies (Jakarta) on March 17, 1630. On May 6 of the same year, it was engaged in a battle against the Portuguese off Djambi (east coast of central Sumatra) and the ship was blown up.

161. **1630** – *OOSTZANEN*, Dutch East Indiaman of 100 tons (captain unknown), arrived in the Indies (Jakarta) on September 21, 1629. On May 6, 1630, while engaged in a battle against the Portuguese off Djambi (east coast of central Sumatra), the ship was blown up.

162. **1677** – *UITDAM*, Dutch East Indiaman of 448 tons, Captain Michiel Kornelisz, arrived in the Indies (Batavia) on August 8, 1671. The ship was wrecked at the island Fortuin near the southern end of Sumatra in November. Today the island is known as Little Fortune Island.

163. **1682** – *GOOILAND*, Dutch East Indiaman of 468 tons, Captain Balthus Groen, arrived in the Indies (Batavia) on June 26, 1673. The vessel later sank at Palembang (southern Sumatra) on September 28, 1682.

164. **1684** – *GELE BEER*, Dutch East Indiaman of 412 tons, Captain Herman Beets, arrived in the Indies (Batavia) on December 7, 1682. The vessel was later wrecked west of Sumatra.

165. **1703** – *MOERKAPELLE*, VOC ship of 685 tons, Captain Willem de Haze, arrived in the Indies (Batavia) on March 16, 1698. The ship was afterwards wrecked on the sands of the river Palembang (on the east coast of southern Sumatra).

166. **1735** – *WENDELA*, Dutch East Indiaman of 600 tons, Captain Pieter Visser, arrived in the Indies (Batavia) on July 31, 1725. The vessel was wrecked on the west coast of Sumatra on February 25.

167. **1758** – *DENHAM*, EIC ship, was burnt and scuttled in the Bengkulu roads (west Sumatra) at latitude 3 degrees 47 minutes north, longitude 102 degrees 15 minutes east in order to prevent capture by the French. Rumoured to have had silver specie on board.

168. **1798** – *HMS RESISTANCE*, British warship, sank on July 24th 14 km (9 miles) off the coast of Palembang while on route to China. The ship had earlier seized several Dutch prizes.

169. **1816** – *UNION*, EIC ship of 400 tons, Captain Barker, was wrecked on Engano Island this year. The inhabitants of the island held the shipwreck victims captive. The ship, *GOOD HOPE* (Captain John Napier), was afterwards dispatched to Engano Island to search for *UNION's* survivors. Captain Barker, the officers and most of the crew died from the cruel treatment received by the savages. Some of the crew were rescued by the *GOOD HOPE*.

170. **1824** – *FAME*, EIC ship, caught fire and sank on 2 February, 80 km (50 miles) southwest of Bengkulu enroute to England. Among the pas-

sengers were Sir Stamford Raffles and his wife. Raffles' entire collection of books, maps and other personal valuables were lost, as well as gold, jewels and a silver plate service presented to him by the Javanese.

171. **1852** – *ARIENIS*, British merchant vessel, was wrecked on Engano Island in this year. The fate of the ship's crew remains unknown.

172. **Year unknown** – *SHAFTSBURY*, ship of unknown origin was lost on a dangerous reef (later named Shaftsbury Reef) which lies in Natal Bay (west coast of Sumatra).

Sumba Island

173. **1817** – *ALICE*, sailing vessel of unknown origin, was wrecked at Sumba Island while on a voyage from Port Louis (Mauritius) to Surabaya (east Java). 850 sovereigns were recovered at the time of loss.

Sunda Straits

The center latitude of this strait is 6 degrees 15 minutes south, longitude 105 degrees 20 minutes east. It is situated between the islands of Sumatra (north) and Java (south).

174. **1629** – *VIANEN*, VOC ship of 400 tons, Captain Albert Dirksz, departed from the Cape of Good Hope on September 12, 1629 bound from Batavia. Upon arrival in the Sunda Straits, the ship was destroyed by fire on November 14.

175. **1637** – *PRINS WILLEM*, Dutch East Indiaman of 500 tons, Captain Laurens Kornelisz Verbeek, departed Batavia on December 29, 1636 for its homeward-bound voyage to the Netherlands. On January 2, the vessel ran ashore in the Sunda Straits off Varkenseiland. Part of the cargo was lost. The crew were saved and the ship broke up. The cargo was valued at 313,514 Dutch florins.

176. **1656** – *MAKREEL*, Dutch East Indiaman of 100 tons (captain unknown), arrived in the Indies (Batavia) on September 16, 1644. The ship sank a few years later in the Sunda Straits.

177. **1697** – *WESTBROEK*, Dutch East Indiaman of 253 tons, Captain Dirk Zalm, arrived in the Indies (Batavia) on August 22, 1685. There the vessel remained until wrecked in the Sunda Straits.

178. **1709** – *KATTENDIJK*, VOC ship of 759 tons, Captain Kornelis de Geus, arrived in the Indies (Batavia) on July 10, 1707. There the vessel remained until wrecked in the Sunda Straits in April.

179. **1716** – *CATHERINE*, EIC ship of 450 tons, Captain Hunter, struck on a sunken rock near Tanjong Ciecorang on September 2 while passing through the south side of the Sunda Straits. The ship bilged but floated off and was run on shore to save the treasure and part of her cargo. The treasure was saved and taken to Batavia in the ship's long boats. The Javanese later burnt the hull of the ship to get the iron.

180. **1731** – *STADHUIS VAN DELFT*, Dutch East Indiaman of 600 tons, Captain Gijsbert Boelen, arrived in the Indies (Batavia) on May 15, 1730. The vessel remained in the Indies until wrecked in the Sunda Straits.

181. **1780** – *ZEEPLOEG*, VOC ship of 1,150 tons, Captain Jan Stil, was on its homeward-bound voyage from China when the vessel was lost in the Sunda Straits. The ship was laden with fine Chinaware. The cargo was valued at 692,863 Dutch florins.

182. **1855** – *VISURAIS*, Oldenburg barque, encountered a storm and was wrecked on the reef to the northwest of Princes Island. None of the cargo was saved.

Ternate
Ternate island is at latitude 0 degrees 47 minutes north, longitude 127 degrees 21 minutes east. It is located a few miles west of Halmahera island.

183. **1608** – *CHINA*, VOC ship of 420 tons, Captain Kornelis Maartensz, was riding at anchor off Ternate in April when the ship was lost during a storm.

184. **1608** – *WALCHEREN*, Dutch East Indiaman of 700 tons, Captain Arend Maartensz, the ship was riding at anchor off Ternate, when the ship was lost.

185. **1682** – *HUIS TE VELSEN*, Dutch East Indiaman of 750 tons (captain unknown), arrived in the Indies (Batavia) on December 14, 1679. There she remained until wrecked on a reef (off Ternate?) on May 22.

Timor Sea
The Timor Sea is located between Timor Island (to the north) and Australia (to the south).

186. **1683** – *HUIS TE NOORWIJK*, VOC ship of 506 tons, Captain Kornelis Jansz de Zeeuw, was wrecked at the Damar Islands on 24 January.

JAPAN

The Japanese archipelago lies off the Asian mainland in an arc at latitude 30 degrees to 40 degrees north. The archipelago consist of over 4,000 islands covering a total land area of 10,990 sq. km. (4,234 sq. miles). The main four large and closely grouped islands (Hokkaido, Honshu, Shikoku and Kyushu) account for 98% of the population. Tokyo was formerly known as Edo.

1. **1573** – Portuguese East Indiaman, was lost off Amakusa Island (near Nagasaki) while on route from China to Japan. Cargo was rumoured to have been gold and porcelain.

2. **1583** – PIE ship that struck and was lost at Ilhas dos Lequios Reef

(Ryukyu Islands) during its voyage from Macao to Japan. Cargo may have been gold and porcelain.

3. **1596** – *SAN FELIPE*, a large Spanish galleon under the command of Matias de Landecho, which departed the Phillipines for Acapulco (Mexico) in July with an unusually valuable cargo and more passengers than ordinary. The ship encountered a succession of storms and the crew was forced to jettison much of the cargo. At latitude 37 degrees, some 150 leagues out of Japan, the vessel lost its rudder. The galleon was badly damaged and appeared in imminent danger of floundering. Rather than turn back, the captain decided to head

An 18th century map of the Sea of Japan

for the unfamiliar coast of Japan. After six days, the Spaniards sighted Shikoku and shortly reached the vicinity of Hirado. A large number of boats came out to the galleon and the locals, in the name of the local *daimio* (chief), urged the Spaniards to come inside the port. The Spaniards consented and allowed the boats to tow the *SAN FELIPE* into the port. However, in the process of towing, the galleon ran into a shoal and her keel was broken. The Spaniards believed that this was intentional as the locals quickly transferred the remaining cargo to shore. Despite strong protests from the Spaniards, the cargo was soon distributed among the villagers and was irretrievably lost.

4. **1599** – Chinese junk disappeared without a trace outside Nagasaki while voyaging from Nagasaki to Macao. Cargo was rumoured to have been silver valued at 400,000 crusados.

5. **1608** – *SAN FRANCISCO*, Spanish galleon, was on a voyage from the Philippines bound for Japan. It was carrying on board the governor of the Philippines and an unusually rich gold consignment. The ship was wrecked off eastern Kyushu. Most of those on board escaped but $2,000,000 in treasure went to the bottom.

6. **1609** – *NOSSA SENHORA DA GRACA* (or *MADRE DE GEOS*), Portuguese East Indiaman which arrived Nagasaki in the late months of the year 1608. In January 1609, the vessel sank outside the port of Nagasaki.

7. **1609** – A heavily laden Spanish galleon (name unknown) which had on board the Spanish interim governor, Don Rodrigo de Vivero y Velasco, was on a voyage from the Philippines to Mexico, was wrecked

in September off the coast of Kazusa in the Kanto area. The ruler of Japan offered the shipwrecked Vivero his own ship so he could continue his voyage to Mexico. Vivero accepted and renamed the Japanese vessel *SAN BUENAVENTURA*. He departed Japan for Mexico on August 1, 1610.

8.   **1616–17** – Spanish ship was lost at south Japan while on route from Manila to Japan.

9.   **1620** – *EXPEDITION*, EIC ship that sank off Firando, NW of Kyushu while voyaging from England to Japan.

10   **1622** – *HOWARD*, VOC ship which sank in Cochie Roads at the port of Firando (NW Kyushu) during its voyage from Bantam (west Java) to Japan.

11. **1622** – *MAAN*, VOC ship which sank in Cochie Roads at the port of Firando (northwestern Kyushu) during its voyage from Bantam (west Java) to Japan.

12. **1663** – *PEPERBAAL*, VOC ship of 510 tons, Captain Vincent Dirksz de Lange, arrived in the Indies (Batavia) on June 7, 1662. The following year on August 26, the vessel was wrecked near Japan (Mishima Islands).

13. **1663** – *VOLLENHOVEN*, Dutch East Indiaman (tonnage unknown), Captain Bastiaan Janz van Nieuwendam, arrived in the Indies (Batavia) on January 17, 1661. Two years later on August 26, the ship was wrecked off Mishima Islands.

14. **1665** – *RODE HERT*, VOC ship of 340 tons, was lost off Nagasaki Bay on August 20th while voyaging from Batavia to Japan.

15. Year **1867** – *SINGAPORE*, British P&O Line vessel, sank 13 km (eight miles) off Hakodate (Japan).

16. **1870** – *ONEIDA*, US Navy corvette, sank on January 24th off Saratoga Spit (Tokyo Bay) about eight km (five miles) from shore. The ship was routed from Yokohama (Japan) to Hongkong. Gold valued at US$50,000 was only rumoured to be on board, but a small quantity of silver was definitely on board.

MALAYSIA

The federation of Malaysia comprises 11 states and a federal territory (Kuala Lumpur) on the Malay peninsula, and two states and a federal territory (Labuan) in northern Borneo. These are separated by some 650 km (400 miles) of sea.

Straits of Malacca

1.   **1509** – Portuguese nau, lost near Malacca (no more than 12 hours sailing out). Captain was perhaps Nuno Godins.

2.   **1519** – Portuguese *lanchara*, lost off Malacca. Cargo consisted mainly of armory.

Remains of the Portuguese fortress, A Formosa, built in 1511. When Malacca was under British adminstration in 1810, there were plans to tear down this remaining gate but this was thankfully halted due to Sir Stamford Raffles's intervention.

3.   **1523** – Portuguese *lancharas* (two of them), under the command of D. Sancho Henriques were lost in April near the Muar river estuary (south of Malacca).

4.   **1583** – Portuguese ship under the command of Coutinho which blew up in a sea battle against the Achinese off Malacca. The vessel was on route from Goa (India) to China.

5.   **1583**   Portuguese carrack that was wrecked on a rock off Johor (south of Malacca) while on a voyage from Goa (India) to Macao. It was rumoured to have had one million crusados for the Chinese silk trade.

6.   **1606** – On August 17, Malacca (which was under Portuguese rule at the time) was besieged by a large Dutch fleet, commanded by Admiral Matalieff de Jonge. The Portuguese fleet consisted of 14 galleons, 4 galleys and 15 or 16 smaller vessels. The Dutch fleet consisted of an unspecified number of galleons and galleys. The two fleets met in a battle off Cape Rachado north of Malacca. After several days of fierce battle, the sunken ship and casualty rates were high. The Portuguese lost four galleons: the *DUARTE DE GUERRA* (burnt), *ALIOZA DE CARUAILLA* (burnt), *GALION SAINT SYMON* (14 pieces of brass cannons were taken by the Dutch who then burnt the vessel) and *SIMON MAU* (burnt), as well as one galley, the *ERASMUS* (eight brass cannons were taken by the Dutch and then the vessel was set on fire). The Dutch lost two galleons: the *MIDDELBURG* and *NASSAU* (both burnt).

In 1993, a salvage group was searching for the lost French vessel,

LA PAIX, off Cape Rachado. They never located the *LA PAIX* but happened upon what may well likely be the final resting place of the above lost warships.

7.   **1606** – *MIDDELBURG* , Dutch East Indiaman of 600 tons, Captain Simon Lambrechtsz Mau, arrived in the Indies (Johor) on May 1, 1606. Three months later on August 18, the ship was burnt in Malacca harbour.

8.   **1620** – *CONCEICAO*, PIE, was lost at an island near the Malacca fortress while on route from Goa to Macao.

9.   **1629** – On July 3, an Achinese fleet commanded by Captain Lassemane (the oldest and bravest captain of the king of Acheh) appeared before Malacca. This fleet consisted of 236 sails, including 38 galleys with two topsails each, the remainder being smaller vessels. At that time, Malacca was on friendly terms with the Sultan of Johor who sent his fleet of 60 sails to assist in Malacca's defence. Together the Portuguese and Johor fleets bombarded the Achinese fleet continually at the Malacca river mouth. By the second day, the Achinese fleet was ruined, with many dead and wounded. Two very large galleons and many smaller ones were also sent to the bottom of the river mouth.

10.   **1636** – A Dutch fleet commanded by Cornelis Symonz Van Der Veer, which consisted of 25 large and small vessels appeared before Malacca in May this year. On the first day, 60 shots were fired at the Portuguese ships. Three Portuguese vessels were sunk from cannon fire. One of them may have been the galleon, *MADRO DI DIOS*, in which 400 men perished, including 96 Portuguese. In this attack, the *WEIRINGEN*, Dutch East Indiaman of 120 tons (captain unknown), caught fire and sank while fighting the Portuguese near Malacca. Only 14 of her crew of 50 survived.

11.   **1642** – *FRANEKER*, VOC ship of 120 tons (captain unknown), arrived in the Indies (Batavia) on June 18, 1639. Three years later on January 18, the ship was lost while fighting against the Portuguese off Malacca.

12.   **1702** – *BAMBEEK*, Dutch East Indiaman of 845 tons, Captain Evert Doedes, arrived in the Indies (Batavia) on November 19, 1700. Two years afterwards on January 1, the ship was wrecked on an uncharted shoal off Cape Rachado on the Malacca coast. Today, this shoal is known as Bambek Shoal.

13.   **1702** – *SPEEDWELL*, Scottish East Indiaman, was lost on a rock in the roads of Malacca in February. Ship was on a voyage from England to China. Most of the cargo was salvaged at the time of loss.

14.   **1787** – Portuguese carrack, was lost in the Straits of Malacca (north of Kelang) during its voyage from Goa to Macao.

15.   **1799** – *CALCUTTA*, English brig that was lost during this year on a rock off the Botel (Bottel) Islands in the Straits of Malacca.

16.   **Year unknown** – *BORNHOLM*, was also lost in the same area as the *CALCUTTA* (see above).

17.   **1805** – *LA PAIX*, French ship, bound from China to Bengal with a cargo

of Chinaware on November 28 was totally lost on Bambek Shoal. The ship was later looted by pirates.

18.   **1806** – A large Portuguese vessel (name unknown) was lost near a point in the Callam Strait known as Anna Garb Point (named after a small sailing vessel called a garb, *ANNA*, which had wrecked there previously). According to an 1841 sailing directions manual, ships were advised to "avoid the wreck of a large Portuguese ship" when passing through this Strait.

19.   **1816** – *CAROLINE*, English (?) ship, bound from Bengal to Canton, was lost on Bambek Shoal.

20.   **1817** – *DIANA*, a British merchant vessel, struck on a reef and sank in the Malacca Straits while on its homeward voyage from Macau to Calcutta. The vessel was laden with 18 tons of Qing dynasty porcelain, none of which was saved at the time. This wreck was located in December 1993 by the salvage group, Malaysian Historical Salvage, off Tanjong Bidara in 32 meters of water. Its cargo of porcelain was salvaged and auctioned for US$2.2 million in March 1995.

21.   **1836** – *ALEXANDER*, grounded and afterwards bilged on South Sands, in the Straits of Malacca.

22.   **1842** (?) – *CAPTAIN BURNEY*, Indian-owned vessel, was wrecked on the Malay coast.

23.   **1843** – *LORD LOWTHER*, English (?) merchant vessel, was lost on the South Sands in the Straits of Malacca.

24.   **1851** – *PACHA*, P&O steamer which collided with the steamer, *ERIN*, off Mount Formosa in the Straits of Malacca and sank shortly afterwards. The P&O steamer had a treasure of specie on board. A salvage team led by and Englishman known as Mr Lovi, searched for the sunken steamer for four years. Finally, some local Malays located it in 20 fathoms of water in May 1855.

      The hull of the sunken vessel appeared to be still intact, with its mast and funnels lying flat on the deck. Strong currents and bad weather hampered the salvage attempts until April 1856, when some of the treasure was eventually recovered by divers. Unfortunately, Mr Lovi suffered from a stroke and died shortly after salvage operations began on the wreck. There is no further mention as to whether all of the treasure was recovered or not.

25.   **1855** – *JOHN CURREY*, was on a voyage from Calcutta to China but was wrecked on the South Sands in the Straits of Malacca on August 28. The vessel was stranded and badly damaged. The ship's crew had to abandon ship and they were brought to Singapore by a passing vessel. *JOHN CURREY* had a cargo of rice.

26.   **1857** – *ANNA ELISABETH*, Dutch ship, was carrying a cargo of rice from Rangoon to Singapore when it wrecked on the North Sands in the Straits of Malacca.

27.   **1857** – *ANTARCTIC*, British ship from Glasgow, Captain Ma Millan,

was on a voyage from Calcutta (India) to Hong Kong (via Singapore). On July 14, at 7.30 p.m., she struck on the South Sands and remained fast. Every effort was made to lighten the ship but all in vain. She gradually settled down in the sand and remained tight. The next day she bilged and filled with water. The captain and crew were taken on board the ship, BENGAL. The ANTARCTIC had on board a valuable cargo of opium, putchuck, rice and general stores. A large part of the cargo was saved and taken to Malacca and was subsequently sold for upwards of $100,000. The ship was reported to have afterwards gone to pieces on the South Sands.

28. **1858** – *CHARLES FORBES*, lost on South Sands.
29. **1858** – *FROLIC*, schooner which sank in a storm off Muar, Johor.
30. **1860** – *SOVEREIGN OF THE SEAS*, merchant ship of 1,000 tons from Liverpool (England), Captain Thomas, was on a voyage from Bombay to China and on the morning of August 7, at 6.20 a.m., was wrecked at Pyramid Shoal in the Straits of Malacca. Attempts were made to get her off and at one time she was afloat with assistance from the schooner *SHIRAZEE*. But a heavy squall struck at that moment and her anchors dragged. She was grounded again and this time showed signs of serious damage. The vessel had a full cargo of cotton, two thousand bales of which were saved and taken to Malacca.

Johor Straits and Johor River

31. **1615** – Portuguese carrack, sank in the Johor Strait at latitude 1 degrees 27 minutes north, longitude 103 degrees 46 minutes east. The ship was routed from India to China with 1,000 souls on board at the time of loss.
32. **1718** – Johor River wrecks, two sloops of unknown origin, were lost in March in the Johor River near Pancor. They were rumoured to have had a cargo of 200 picals (12,000 kg or 27,000 lbs) of gold and many other valuable items belonging to Sultan Raiamuda of Johor.

East Coast of Peninsular Malaysia

33. **1670** – *VREDENBURG*, VOC ship of 160 tons (captain unknown), was wrecked and burnt on Poulo Timaon (Tioman Island) on July 7.
34. **1726** – *RISDAM*, Dutch East Indiamen of 520 tons, Captain Kornelis Dam, sank on a voyage from Siam to Batavia.

Portuguese carracks were the earliest European sailing ships to come to Southeast Asia.

MYANMAR (BURMA)

Myanmar's borders touch five other Asian countries: Bangladesh, India, China, Laos and Thailand. It has over 700 miles of coastline with hundreds of islands dotting the Andaman Sea. Total land area is 676,550 sq. km. (261,216 sq. miles).

1. **1661** – KONING DAVID, Dutch East Indiaman of 600 tons, Captain Konnelis Rob, sunk at Pegu in April this year. Ten men were drowned.
2. **1681** – DEN BRIEL, Dutch East Indiaman of 766 tons, Captain Theunis Andriesz, was wrecked at Arrakan (north Myanmar coast) on October 20, 1681.
3. **1766** – FALMOUTH, EIC ship of 499 tons, was wrecked on a shoal off the coast of Arrakan on June 13. The vessel was totally lost and every one perished.
4. **1808** – TRAVERS, EIC ship of 577 tons, bound for the Bay of Bengal, was totally lost on November 7 at 5 a.m. after striking on a sunken rock near Alguada Reef (near Diamond Island).
5. **1825** – JANET HUTTON, English (?) ship, was wrecked on a sandbar near the entrance of the Rangoon River.
6. **1860** – CALCUTTA, a British India Steam Navigation Company ship of 527 tons, was lost on Arklow Bank only a few hours after leaving from the builder's yard.
7. **1868** – ETHIOPIA, Indian-owned steamship of 1,126 tons, was wrecked off the Burma coast.
8. **1882** – SOCOTRA, Indian-owned steamship of 1,947 tons, was wrecked off the Burma coast.

NEW GUINEA

The western half of this island, Irian Jaya, forms part of Indonesia and the eastern half is the independent state of Papua New Guinea. Its center is at approximately latitude 5 degrees south, longitude 141 degrees east.

1. **1719** – INDIAN QUEEN, (origin unknown) of 250 tons and 28 guns, commanded by Captain Oliver de la Bouche, was bound from the Guinea coast to the East Indies and was bilged and lost.
2. **During or after 1747** – DIEMERMEER, Dutch East Indiaman of 850 tons (captain unknown), was wrecked during or after 1747 off the coast of Guinea.
3. **1783** – ANTELOPE PACKET, EIC ship of 270 tons and eight guns, Captain Henry Wilson, departed Macau on July 20 and was wrecked on or near one of the Pelew Islands three weeks later. There were no casualties. After some time, another boat was built and the shipwrecked crew made passage to Macau at the beginning of December.

It was the ship's maiden voyage.

4. **1826** – *SUN*, 185 ton brig (origin unknown), was lost somewhere in the vicinity of the Gulf of Papau during its voyage from Sydney, (Australia) to Jakarta (west Java). It is rumoured that the brig had specie to the value of Spanish $40,000.

5. **1853** – *JACK*, brig, was wrecked on the northeast point of the Great Detached Shoal of the Barrier Reef.

6. **1854** – *ART VAN NES*, a Dutch vessel, wrecked on the Great Detached Reef (Torres Strait entrance) on April 17. The vessel was a total loss and the crew were obliged to abandon it immediately. Eighteen days later they were plundered of everything they had by nine pirate *proas*, stripping them of all clothing, food and even the hats on their heads. They then suffered from hunger and exposure to heat and cold, wind and rain. On May 26, they managed to land at the east coast of the Celebes (Sulawesi) where they were treated kindly by the local *rajah* (king).

7. **1854** – In June of this year, the *Singapore Free Press* reports the loss of several Dutch ships in the Torres Strait (no names mentioned).

8. **1855** – *PHOENIX*, wrecked in the Torres Strait.

9. **1858** – *BLACK SWAN*, Rotterdam ship, Captain Stikkel, was lost in the Torres Strait in June 21. The captain and 11 seamen arrived safely at Timor Koepang on the ship's boat on July 11.

10. **1890** – *QUETTA*, Indian-owned steamship of 3,302 tons, was wrecked in the Torres Strait.

NORTH CHINA SEA

This covers the region located between Taiwan and Japan.

1. **1613** – *RODE LEEUW*, VOC ship of 400 tons, Captain Volert Thijsz, while sailing from Manilla was lost near Japan on January 31.

2. **1653** – *SPERWER*, Dutch East Indiaman of 540 tons (captain unknown), arrived in the Indies (Batavia) on December 28, 1648. The ship remained in the Indies and was lost on August 16, while sailing from Taiwan to Japan.

PHILIPPINES

The archipelago of the Philippines consists of 7,107 islands, of which 2,770 are named and only 1,000 permanently inhabited. Its land area covers 300,000 sq. km. (115,300 sq. miles). The two largest islands, Luzon and Mindanao, make up over two-thirds of the total area.

1. **1576** – *ESPIRITU SANTO*, Acapulco galleon, went to pieces on the

Catanduanes and all on board were either drowned or killed by the natives upon reaching shore. She was carrying a large company of soldiers and many friars out to the islands.

2. **1578** – *SAN JUANILLO*, Spanish galleon of 300 tons, under the command of Juan de Ribera, departed from Manilla bound for Acapulco with a cargo of about $750,000 in oriental products, including at least $150,000 in gold. The ship headed east into the San Bernadino Straits and was never heard of again.

3. **1589** – Two partly loaded Spanish galleons (names unknown), sank in Cavite port. There is little record of their cargo or whether they were salvaged.

4. **1590** – *SAN FELIPE*, *Almiranta* of the Armada from Acapulco, was wrecked on a reef of Marinduque Island (Philippines) near shore. The crew got to safety and her cargo, which included over $500,000 in silver, was partly saved.

Map of Luzon island in the Philippines. Many of the Manilla galleons sank to their watery grave in this region.

5. **1596** – *SAN JERONIMO*, Spanish galleon, Captain Fernando de Castro, was laden and returning from a four month trip from Mexico to the Philippines. Late in June, with Luzon almost in sight, the ship was dashed against the reefs of Cataduanes where she broke up. Captain de Castro and nearly the whole crew were wiped out while 1,500,000 silver minted pesos sank onto the rocky shoal. There is no record of this treasure being salvaged.

6. **1600** – *SAN PABLO*, Spanish galleon, was wrecked on the Ladrones.

7. **1600** – *SAN DIEGO*, Spanish *patache* out of Manilla, was in a sea battle on December 14 against a fleet of Dutch ships (led by Admiral Oliver van Noort). The Spanish put up a brave battle against the superior enemy ships, fighting to the end. When the little *patache* sank, most of her crew were already wounded or dead. Aboard this ship was probably a small quantity of gold and silver. (This wreck was excavated and salvaged in 1993 by the European Institute of Underwater Archeology jointly with the National Museum of the Philippines).

8. **1601** – *SANTO TOMAS*, Acapulco galleon, was wrecked on the Catanduanes off the east coast of Luzon. Her crew got ashore with most of her cargo and very little silver was lost.

9. **1603** – *NESTRA SENORA DE LA REMEDIOS*, Spanish galleon, was lost near Manila during its return voyage from Acapulco. Silver specie would have been on board.

10. **1603** – *SAN ANTONIO*, Spanish galleon, which, according to the ship's crew, not only carried on her "the greatest wealth of any galley up to that time" but also had on board many of the first citizens of the city who were "fleeing from the troubles of Manilla" with their families. This galley left Manilla Bay and was never heard from again.

11. **1610** – *AREND*, Dutch East Indiamen of 140 tons, Captain Rutger Thomasz, was captured and burnt by the Spaniards off Manilla on April 25.

12. **1613** – A squadron of six Spanish war galleons (names unknown), commanded by Admiral Heredia, headed south from Cavite to reinforce Spanish and Portuguese under attack by the Dutch in the Moluccas (Indonesia). As the squadron passed through the Mindoro Canal, they met with a typhoon. All six galleons were wrecked or sunk in the passage.

13. **1617** – *GROTE AEOLUS*, VOC ship of 320 tons, Captain Job Kornelisz, arrived in the Indies (Ternate) on March 30, 1616. The following year, on April 16, the ship exploded in a battle off Manilla.

14. **1617** – *GROTE ZON*, Dutch East Indiamen of 600 tons, Captain Reinier Jansz, arrived in the Indies (Ternate) on March 30, 1616. The following year, on April 16, the ship exploded in the battle of Manilla.

15. **1617** – *NIEUWE SONNE*, VOC ship of 320 tons, was burnt during a sea engagement with the Spanish near Wittert's Island (north of Manila Bay) on April 16th.

16. **1617** – *TER VEERE*, Dutch East Indiamen of 320 tons, blew up during a sea engagement with the Spanish near Wittert's Island (north of Manila Bay) on April 16th.

17. **1620** – *JESUS MARIA*, Spanish galleon, was returning from Acapulco through the San Bernardino Straits (under the south coast of Luzon) and was ambushed by a waiting Dutch fleet. A violent battle was fought all day in which the greatly out numbered Spaniards held off the Dutch until their ship was a battered wreckage and their casualties numerous. Late in the afternoon, the ship settled into the sea of the San Bernardino Straits with her 460-man crew. The ship had on board about $1,000,000 silver pesos. The silver was saved.

18. **1620** – *SANTA ANA*, Spanish galleon, Captain Pedro Alvarez Piger, was returning from Acapulco through the San Bernardino Straits (under the south coast of Luzon) and was ambushed by a waiting Dutch fleet. A violent battle was fought all day in which the greatly out numbered Spaniards held off the Dutch until their ship was a battered wreckage and their casualties numerous. At dusk, Captain Piger surrendered. However, it was too late as most of the crew were dead and the galleon was already damaged beyond repair. During

the night, it was stranded on sand in the San Bernardino Straits. Her treasure of about $1,000,000 silver pesos was probably saved.

19. **Late 1620** – *SAN NICOLAS*, Spanish galleon, accompanied by a *patache*, was returning from Acapulco through the San Bernadino Straits (under the south coast of Luzon) and was ambushed by a waiting Dutch fleet. A running battle down the Samar coast broke out and the Spaniards were still fighting back strongly when, under cover of the night, they broke away and escaped. The captain of the *SAN NICOLAS* decided to anchor in the nearby Bay of Borongan to repair damage. But a wind came up, the ship's mooring ropes parted and she drifted on to the rocks near the shore. Her crew got off safely and the silver was carried ashore. A few days later, the *patache* was wrecked at Palapag but its cargo was also salvaged.

20. **1621** – *NUESTRA SENORA DE VIDA*, Spanish galleon, was wrecked due to an incompetent pilot. He had only taken the galleon as far as Isla Verde between Luzon and Mindoro when the ship hit a reef. The ship had to be abandoned to the waves. The pilot was promptly hanged on the nearby shore by the infuriated passengers.

21. **1631** – *MADALENA*, Spanish galleon, sank in Cavite harbour during a storm. Some cargo and 14 people were lost.

‡ *MADALENA*, Spanish galleon, just as she was ready to clear port, the ship turned over on her side at her moorings before Cavite.

22. **1637** – *CAPITANA DE ESPANA*, a junk built on the lines of the Chinese ships and used for inter-island trading was wrecked in the Philippines. Two of her crew were drowned and possibly some gold lost.

23. **1638** – *RIJNSBURG*, Dutch East Indiaman of 200 tons (captain unknown), arrived in the Indies (Batavia) on April 28, 1638. The ship remained in the Indies and was later lost in action against the Spaniards near the Philippines.

24. **1639** – *CHAMPAN*, Spanish ship that was lost 19 kilometres (12 miles) from Manila while on route from Manila to China.

25. **1639** – *SAN AMBROSIO*, Spanish galleon and another ship from Acapulco, were smashed against the coast of Cagayan during a typhoon. One hundred and fifty people were drowned and over $2,000,000 silver pesos were smashed against the rocks below. The governor later recovered all of this treasure with the help of local divers.

26. **1643** – *BUEN JESUS*, Acapulco galleon, was lost during this year.

27. **1646** – *SAN LUIS*, Spanish galleon, under the command of General Fernando Lopez Perona, was arriving from Acapulco and got stranded on the reefs off the Cagayan coast. Her crew, silver and other cargo were saved.

28. **1649** – *ENCARNATION*, Manilla galleon, was late coming from Acapulco and crashed on the Sorsogon coast of Luzon near Bulan.

29. **1653** – *SAN FRANCISCO JAVIER*, Spanish galleon, with General Lorenzo

de Ugalde aboard, was shipwrecked in the Philippines.

30. **1654** – *SAN DIEGO*, Spanish galleon, sank in Manilla Bay. There were no casualties or loss of treasure.

31. **1658** – *BRUINVIS*, Dutch East Indiaman of 120 tons (captain unknown), arrived in the Indies (Batavia) on October 17, 1645. The ship remained in the Indies and was blown up on January 20 off Maginado by the Spaniards or by the ship's crew.

32. **1658** – *WILLIAM*, English East Indiaman, went down in sight of Manilla port while coming from India. Route was India to Manilla.

33. **1660** – *VICTORIA*, Spanish warship, while on route from Manilla to Zamboanga, the ship floundered with a loss of all hands and treasure on board.

34. **1678** – *TREVITORE*, EIC ship, was lost on September 4th near the southwest coast of Mindanao Island during its voyage from Madras (India) to Manila.

35. **1679** – *SAN ANTONIO DE PADUA*, Manilla galleon, lost during this year.

36. **1693** – *SANTO CRISTO DE BURGOS*, Spanish galleon, disappeared east of Luzon shortly after departing from Manilla with $1,000,000 treasure of Far East exports. She or her crew were never heard of again. Her gold, pearls, ivory, and gems went to the bottom of the sea with her.

‡ *SANTA CRISTO*, Spanish galleon, was struck by a storm on the night of July 3, 1694 while going out through the *boca* of Marivels. The ship was broken to pieces on the island of Lubang almost opposite the entrance of Manilla Bay.

37. **1694** – *SAN JOSE*, Spanish galleon, was dashed to pieces on Lubang Island off Manilla Bay during a typhoon. She had on board a full cargo and a crew of 400. All the crew were drowned. Her hull lies in shallow water. Somewhere in the ballast of rocks should be a fortune in precious metal.

‡ *SAN JOSE*, Spanish galleon, was struck by a storm on the night of July 3, 1694 while going out through the *boca* of Marivels. The ship was broken to pieces on the island of Lubang almost opposite the entrance of Manilla Bay. She was the largest galleon built. Over 400 people drowned and a cargo of more that 12,000 *piezas* or packages were lost. "No larger or richer galleon had ploughed the sea", wrote Padre Casimiro Diaz, "for the wealth that she carried was incredible". (This galleon was located and excavated in 1985).

38. **1705** – *SAN FRANCISCO JAVIER*, Spanish galleon, departed Cavite for the long voyage to America and was never heard from again. She was carrying on board the usual export cargo.

39. **1726** – *SANTO CRISTO DE BURGOS*, Spanish galleon, which, a few days after leaving Manilla Bay, was grounded near the shore of Ticao Island in the Philippines. Among other items, she had on board gold, gems and ivory from Siam (Thailand) and the Far East. Although the

crew and passengers were saved, the cargo and the ship was destroyed by fire and much of her treasure was lost.

40. **1729** – *NUESTRA SENORA DE LOS DOLORES*, Spanish patache which was lost near the town of Abulu (Mindanao Island) while on route from Manila to Acapulco.

41. **1730** – *SACRA FAMILIAS*, Spanish ship, was lost at the Embocadero, San Bernadino Strait, during its voyage from Acapulco (Mexico) to Manila. The vessel would most probably have had silver specie on board.

42. **1734** – *SANTA MARIA MADALENA*, Spanish galleon, which was crammed with cargo until the waterline reached the dangerous level, and still more merchandise was loaded in her upper hold. When the galleon finally set sail from Cavite, she capsized and sank a few hundred yards from her anchorage in Manilla Bay. It is likely that her treasure was salvaged.

43. **1735** – *SAN CHRISTOBAL*, Manilla galleon, ran onto the Calantas shoals near Bulusan.

44. **1735** – A small *patache* (name unknown), struck on the Calantas Reef near Bulusan. As the shipwreck location was known, salvors were able to recover 1,518,000 silver pesos before the work was abandoned. However, a large quantity still remains beneath the waves.

45. **1741** – *NUESTRA SENORA DE LA GUIA*, Manilla galleon, vanished after departing from Manilla Bay.

46. **1750** – *PILAR*, Manilla galleon, Captain Ignacio Martinez, claimed to have been lost due to the bull-headedness of the captain. The ship started leaking even before she had cleared Corregidor in Manilla Bay. Passengers and crew begged Captain Martinez to return and he was reported to have roared, "To Acapulco or purgatory!". The galleon never reached Acapulco. Drowned bodies and debris from the ship drifted onto the eastern coast of Luzon, indicating that the galleon had sank nearby. She was carrying two million pesos in coin.

47. **1756** – *CAPITANA*, Manilla galleon, Captain Pedro Vertiz, sank upon arrival at the Cataduanes, off the San Bernadino Strait, from her Acapulco voyage. All but a handful of survivors were lost. This galleon probably carried two million silver pesos but lies in deep water.

48. **1756** – *LA GALERA*, Spanish ship, was lost off Catanduanes (central east Philippines) during its voyage from Manila to Acapulco.

49. **1761** – *GRIFFIN*, EIC ship of 499 tons, Captain Dethick, was on a homeward voyage from China in company with three other EIC vessels, *VALENTINE*, *POCOCK* and *OXFORD*, when the ship struck a reef on the night of January 21 near Soloo in the Philippines. The vessel floated off the jagged reef and sank in deeper water before any of its cargo could be saved by the three nearby ships. The sunken cargo included 125,800 pieces of Chinaware and other Far Eastern goods.

This ship was located and excavated in 1986. Several thousand pieces of Chinese ceramics and artifacts were recovered.

50. **1762** – Acapulco galley (name unknown), under Filipino command, was run ashore and wrecked on the Navotas on September 24, while being chased by English East Indiamen. The captain and some passengers were taken prisoners. Not being able to get the galley off the reef, the English then stripped it of everything valuable and set it on fire.

51. **1773** – *ROYAL CAPTAIN*, EIC ship of 1,200 tons, Captain Edward Berrow, was on its homeward journey from China and struck a hidden shoal in the Sulu Sea. The vessel sank in deeper water shortly after. None of the cargo of fine Chinese porcelain and other valuables were saved. Today, this reef bears the vessel's name (The Royal Captain Shoal). An expedition in 1985 failed to locate the final resting place of this vessel but eventually succeeded in locating another lost EIC ship, the *GRIFFIN* (see above).

52. **1782** – *SAN PEDRO*, Manilla galleon, lost north of Luzon.

53. **1797** – *MARIA*, Spanish frigate, Commander Fernando Quintano, sank during a typhoon on the night of April 24 off Cape Bojeador. Commander Quintano, 13 officers and 322 men were lost with the vessel.

54. **1797** – Early in May, the Spaniards encountered a typhoon in which every ship was dismasted and one frigate (name not mentioned) lost. The survivors returned to Manilla.

55. **1798** – *SAN ANDRES*, Manilla galleon, Commanded by Manuel Lecoraz, was wrecked on the Naranjos Shoals near Ticao after leaving Manilla for Mexico. The people on board this galleon were saved but part of her valuable cargo could not be taken off in time.

56. **1808** – *TELLICHERRY*, Botany Bay ship, was lost on Apo Shoal in the Mindoro Strait. The vessel was on a voyage from Australia to China.

57. **1816** – *COUNTESS OF LONDON*, English ship, Captain Hammond, was on a voyage from Bengal (India) to China and was lost early in November upon a shoal off Palawan Island. The ship struck in the night and soon filled with water and sank. The vessel *SUSAN* was travelling in company and saved the crew of the *COUNTESS OF LONDON*.

58. **1821** – *FIDELIDAD*, Spanish ship, sank off of Lubang island.

59. **1822** – *REGENT*, English East Indiaman of 916 tons, was on a voyage from Canton to the Philippines when it was stranded on route. The ship was loaded with English woolens and their loss was considered almost valueless to the East India Committee in Canton.

‡ **1822** – *REGENT*, was sailing through the Palawan Passage and at dawn on October 12th, struck a shoal southwest of Palawan Island. The ship lost its steering rudder and was afterwards totally wrecked.

60. **1827** – *ASIA*, (origin unknown), was lost off of Lubang island on October 24th. A salvage attempt which involved Captain Campbell

of the CYRENE is thought to have been unsuccessful.

61. **1841** – SULTANA, (origin unknown), sank on January 4th some 50 kilometers (30 miles) northeast of Bombay Shoal (off Palawan's east coast). Some of the cargo of specie and jewels were later salvaged.

62. **1852** – OHIO, German ship, sank in November between Catanduanes and the San Bernadino Strait during its voyage from Lima (Peru) to China. Some of the ship's specie was salvaged shortly after its loss.

63. **1856** – JOHANNA MARIA, Dutch merchant vessel, Captain de Jong, struck on a reef in the Solo Sea and sank on March 23. Captain de Jong drowned. The mate and the crew, consisting of 14 men, embarked on two boats and nine days afterwards landed on Point Maria (Mindanao Island). Here they were plundered of all they had by pirates who then took them prisoner. They were soon afterwards ransomed for $2,000 Spanish dollars and sent to Sambonga. After remaining there for seven days, they were forwarded to Manilla on the Spanish steamer, MAGELANES.

64. **1859** – REINDEER, American clipper ship, was wrecked on February 12th on a coral reef near the town of Iba, Luzon (north of Olongapo city). Scheduled route was Manila to San Francisco (California). It is rumoured that the ship had some gold on board.

65. **1868** – CHINA PACKET, American ship, sank on August 4th off Cabanatuan (central east Luzon) while on route from California to Hongkong.

66. **1891** – RAINBOW, English ship, was lost on October 31st at approximate latitude 20 degrees north, longitude 120 degrees east (Luzon Strait).

SINGAPORE

The Republic of Singapore island's center lies at latitude 1 degrees 27 minutes north, longitude 103 degrees 50 minutes east. It comprises the main island and an additional 54 smaller islands lying within its territorial waters. The total land area is 618 sq. km. (239 sq. miles). Singapore is also known as Singapura and was formerly known as Temasek.

1. **1578** – On January 1, a sea battle took place off Changi Point between a large Portuguese and Achinese fleet. The Portuguese fleet was commanded by Captain Mathias de Albuquerque (descendent of Alfonso) and consisted of 18 sails (three high-sided vessels, three galleys, seven foists and a China junk). The Achinese fleet consisted of 150 sails which included several large Achinese galleys (built by renegade Portuguese), all well armed with spheres and basilisks which "fired a shot as large as a man's head", according to the Portuguese crew. A fierce battle broke out with both sides firing shots

with considerable fury for six hours. Many of the smaller Achinese ships and at least one of the galleys, the vice admiral's, was burnt and sunk during this battle. Casualties included 13 Portuguese and 1,600 Achinese.

2. **1583** – Portuguese carrack, under the command of Simao Ferreira, sank in January between Bedok and Changi Point (southeast Singapore). The ship was routed from Malacca to China and was rumoured to have been carrying a large quantity of silver crusados (some of which were later salvaged).

The top of Fullerton lighthouse that once beamed upon Singapore's busy harbour, now on display at the Maritime Museum, Singapore.

3. **1796** – *SHAH MUNSHY* (or *SHAH MUNCHAN*), a large and valuable ship from Bombay, was lost on the rocks of Pedra Branca on January 8. The ship was bound from China to Bombay. The crew managed to get in the boats safely, but the ship soon afterwards went to pieces on the rocks and none of the cargo was saved.

4. **1830** – Chinese junk, sailing from Singapore to Shanghai (China) was wrecked in July near Pedra Branca rock. Supposedly on board was a cargo of specie worth $22,016.

5. **1836** – *PASCOA*, Indian-owned vessel, was wrecked near Singapore.

6. **1857** – *ZARAH*, barque of Jersey, was leaving the Singapore port for Akyab (Myanmar) on January 1, and was run into by the screw steamer *LABUAN*. She sank within three minutes, the crew barely having time to get on board the *LABUAN*. The barque owners later brought the suit to court to try and get compensation for their lost vessel from the Eastern Archipelago Company (owners of the *LABUAN*). The amount claimed was $32,423, being the value of the barque and the treasure on board.

7. **1857** – *CALEDONIA*, French barque, was burnt and sank while at anchor in the Singapore roads.

8. **1857** – *PINANG*, Singapore barque, left Singapore on the morning of September 13 bound for Malacca and Pinang. There were 65 persons on board, including passengers and crew. At 8.30 p.m. she was caught by a tremendous squall which threw her on her beam ends, and before she could right, she came within the vortex of a waterspout and sank altogether. Some of the survivors were picked up by a passing boat while floating on the ship's wreckage. This ship was

presumed lost somewhere in the vicinity of Raffles Lighthouse.

9.   **1862** – BUSSORAH, Indian-owned vessel of 622 tons, was lost with all hands in the North Channel (Singapore Strait) during this year.

SOUTH CHINA SEA

Paracel Islands

The geographical position of these islands is between latitude 15 degrees 46 minutes and 17 degrees 8 minutes north, and longitude 111 degrees 11 minutes and 112 degrees 54 minutes east. The archipelago consists of 15 islets covering a total land area of about 3 sq. km. with more than a dozen partly or temporarily submerged reefs and banks, scattered over an area forming a large oval of about 200 km.

The Paracel Islands are claimed by the following countries: the People's Republic of China, Republic of China (Taiwan) and the Republic of Vietnam. In January 1974, a military conflict broke out between China and Vietnam in the Paracels in which China was the victor. As a result, the whole archipelago is now under China's control.

1.   **1690** – Portuguese East Indiaman which struck and was lost at the north Paracel Islands during its voyage from Goa (India) to Macao.

2.   **1714** – ARION, VOC ship of 630 tons, was lost in the Paracel Islands during its voyage from Batavia to Japan.

3.   **1759** – EARL TEMPLE, British trading vessel, struck on one of the south Paracel Islands and afterwards lost. It was routed from Batavia to Manila.

4.   **1801** – GENEROUS FRIENDS, ship of unknown origin, was wrecked on November 2nd on a reef in the Paracels after two days sailing distance southwest by south from Macao. The cargo of gold and US dollars was plundered by pirates.

The treacherous Paracel Shoals were the scene of many shipwrecks.

5.   **1804** – SAINT ANTONIA, Portuguese ship of Macau, departed Canton on July 20 and the following day, a gale commenced from a northwest direction outside the Gulf

of Tonkin which increased to a violent storm. Not being able to carry sail, she was driven leeward and wrecked upon one of the shoals in the Paracel group. The commander and part of the crew later reached Hanian Island on a raft, from whence they were re-conveyed to Canton.

6.   **1837** – *JOHN BANNERMAN*, English ship, Captain Wilson, left Lintin on December 17 bound for Cochin China and Bombay (India). During a hard gale, the ship lost her main and mizzen topmasts and about midnight on December 18, she struck on the North Shoal (Reef) of the Paracels (at latitude 17 degrees 5 minutes, longitude 111 degrees 25 minutes). The ship appeared to have broken its back and she began to take in water rapidly. The captain, chief officer and 18 seamen left the wreck, leaving 85 of the crew on board as nothing could be done to save them. After four days, the boat reached the coast of Cochin China. Several of the crew had perished along the route while others died of exhaustion. (There is no mention as to what happened to the 85 crew members left on the wrecked vessel).

‡   **Year unknown** – *JOHN BANNERMAN*, Surat (India) built vessel, was wrecked on the Paracel's Reef, South China Sea.

7.   **1845** – *CASTLE HUNTLEY*, British ship, struck on Lincon's Shoal in the Paracel group on October 27th and lost shortly afterwards.

8.   **During or after 1855** – *DOURO*, P&O Company steamship, was disabled by a typhoon in the China Sea. The ship drifted out of control and grounded on the desolate islands of the Paracel group, 200 miles from the nearest land in the South China Sea. Two officers patched up a boat and sailed it over 400 miles to Hong Kong for help for the remainder of the crew and passengers.

9.   **1857** – *VONDELLE*, Dutch barque, lost near the Paracels in a heavy typhoon. The ship's captain and crew arrived safely at Singapore (from Macau) on November 17.

10. **1858** – *ANTELOPE*, American ship of New York, Captain Clarke, left the outer anchorage of Bangkok on August 27, bound for China. On September 5, observations were taken which made the ship about 70 miles distance from Discovery Shoal. On the following morning at about 6:45 a.m., the ship struck fast on a shoal. After several chronometer positions were taken (they proved to be correct), it left no doubt in the captain's mind that the current had sent the ship 40 miles out of her course in the last 18 hours.

   Immediately after the ship struck, the anchor was let down but no bottom could be found from the stern of the ship. The tide was decidedly falling soon after the ship struck, and the cargo was jettisoned in hopes of re-floating the ship. This, however, proved to be in vain for the tide continued falling until there was only three feet of water remaining under the vessel. The entire shoal then became visible. Its shape was elliptical, about eight miles in diameter one way and six in the other. With the wind and seas, all hopes of saving the ship were abandoned.

At 6 p.m. the crew took to their boats, in hopes of safely clearing the reefs before sunset. They took no arms as they were under the idea that they might cause trouble and could do no good (this was later found to be a fatal mistake). The shipwreckers were in two boats, 18 persons to a boat, including the captain, and the first mate and nine more in the other. The intention was to keep together and make for the nearest land which was a place on the charts called Leong Soey on the coast of Hanian.

Unfortunately the boats parted company and nothing further was heard of the first mate's boat. The captain's boat made the high land of Hanian on the September 9 and met with two fishing boats. The fishermen seemed to have a friendly nature and agreed to tow the ANTELOPE's crew to a place where water might be obtained for some money. A line was made fast but instead of towing the boat towards the shore, the fishermen began to go in a circle. They then demanded more money. A second boat of fishermen came and it was clear that their intentions were hostile. Captain Clark then made off under sail and oar and managed to get away. Night fell. The following morning on September 11, upon rounding an island, they saw three fishing boats bearing down on them, obviously with unfriendly intentions. Trying to elude them, the first Chinese boat ran into their stern, carrying away their rudder. The Chinese were armed with spears and knifes. Under these circumstances, everything was surrendered to them and passed out of the boat over the stern. The sight of the plunder was too much for the Chinese and they relaxed their guard. Upon seeing this, two sturdy seamen sprung onto the Chinese boat's deck, Captain Clark immediately afterwards, overpowering the pirates and killing them. The other two Chinese boats made off immediately upon seeing the state of affairs. Only one man of the ANTELOPE's crew was wounded and all the property was recovered. Two days later, they arrived safely at port. The ANTELOPE had been chartered to carry a valuable cargo of opium, valued at upwards of $100,000.

11.   **1859** – *FLORA TEMPLE*, American merchant ship of 1,915 tons, Captain Johnson, left Macau for Havana (Cuba) on Saturday morning, October 8, 1859. She had a crew of 50 and 850 Chinese coolies. Three days out of Macau at 7 a.m., a group of coolies had collected on deck in large numbers. Unknown to the captain and crew, they were planning to murder them and take possession of the ship. Suddenly they fell upon the guard at the starboard gate, struck him on the head with an iron baylaying pin as he was stooping down, drew out his sword and cut him down with cruel ferocity. While this was going on, some of the other coolies were calling "fire, fire!" to induce the watch, who

were in the front part of the ship, to go down to the decks below. They then made a rush through the barricade towards the cabins, arming themselves with anything they could get their hands on.

Fortunately, the captain had come on the poop and saw what was going on. He immediately ran to his cabin and seized his revolver. At the same time, the remainder of the crew were also arming themselves. After firing several unexpected shots from revolvers, the frenzied coolies were brought under control. However, one of the crew was hacked to death and several others wounded.

After the mutiny attempt by the coolies, it was impossible for the captain and crew to place any trust in them thereafter and they were constantly on guard.

All went well until the night of October 14 at 7.30 p.m., when the ship's lookout suddenly shouted, "hard up!" The helm was instantly put hard up and the spanker lowered. In fact, the ship was already within a very short distance of the breakers. Although the yards were braced round and the ship hove aback, she struck the shoal, first slightly but crashed hard several more times after. The breakers were running very high alongside. Pieces of timber and planking floated up on her port side. After some more hard bumps, the FLORA TEMPLE remained fast, apparently immovable with a heavy list to port. The water had rapidly increased from two and one half feet in the well, till it reached the between decks where the coolies were. It was impossible to extricate her.

With this going on, the captain and crew feared that the coolies would rise and murder all on board. When the two life boats were lowered, only the officers and crew were allowed first. The life boat crew had orders to remain close to the ship. A few of these managed to get through the breakers safely. Fifteen were all that remained of the crew still on board the FLORA TEMPLE.

The ship appeared to be stationary – all her masts were standing, she had a strong list to port and her back was broken. Amidship, the sea was making a clear breech over her starboard quarter. The coolies, who had remained below all night, were now up and clustered on the upper decks. Due to the circumstances, the captain felt that there was nothing more that he could do to help the coolies so he proceeded in one of the boats back towards the China coast. On the 14th

Report of the FLORA TEMPLE, wrecked on the Paracel Islands.

day from the wreck, after going through gale, rough seas, exposure and much difficulties, the captain and 30 other crew members arrived at Touron, a French settlement at Cochin China. There they were immediately received on board the HIM French steamer, *GIRONDE*. The other two life boats with crew were never heard of again, presumed perished at sea in the severe storm.

The *GIRONDE* was dispatched with orders to return to the wreck site of the *FLORA TEMPLE*. On Wednesday afternoon, November 2, they sighted the reef again. Unrelenting seas still rolled and broke as before, but there was no sign of the ship. On a closer look from on a small boat, only the port side of the *FLORA TEMPLE* from the mainchains forward could be seen floating attached to the remainder by the rigging, together with what seemed to be the mainsky-sail mast. There was no trace of the 850 Chinese coolies.

On today's charts this reef is known as Western or Flora Temple Reef and is located at latitude 10 degrees 15 minutes north, longitude 113 degrees 37 minutes east.

12. **1862** – *EMMA*, American ship, Captain Sherman, totally lost on the Paracels on February 13 at 4.30 a.m., two days after departing from Macau, with great loss of life. The vessel struck aft at low water and immediately broke in half. Many of the men refused to leave the wreck and were killed or drowned when the bowsprit and fore part of the ship fell in. Captain Sherman and two of his crew were last seen in a long boat, drifting out to sea. The chief officer, five of the crew, and 22 Chinese passengers managed to get to Amphitrite island, where they remained for 55 days. They were then brought to Singapore (from Amphitrite island) on another vessel for the sum of $2,000.

13. **1863** – *HOTSPUR*, American ship, 862 tons, lost on Paracel's Reef.

14. **1871** – *YANGZEE*, American tea clipper ship, was lost in the vicinity of the Paracel Islands while on route from New York to Fuzhou (China).

Pratas Shoals

The geographical position of this shoal is between latitude 20 degrees 30 minutes and 21 degrees 30 minutes north, longitude 116 degrees and 117 degrees east. Pratas island is 6 km long and 2 km wide and is totally surrounded by a large submerged shoal of about 18 km in diameter. The island is located on the westernmost part of the shoal. It is claimed by China and Taiwan but has been in Taiwan's control for some time.

15. **1609** – Portuguese East Indiaman was wrecked on an uninhabited island between Macao and Manila (Philippines) that was thought to be Dongsha Qundao Reef (Pratas Shoal) while on route from Macao to Manila. Cargo was rumoured to have been amber, musk, pearls and precious stones.

16. **1654** – *UTRECHT*, Dutch East Indiaman that was lost on June 22nd after striking Dongsha Quandao Reef (Pratas Shoal) while on route from Batavia to China. One chest of silver was saved.

17. **1761** – *FREDERIC ALDOLPHUS*, SEI of 974 tons and 28 guns (cannons), was bound for China in company with the SEI vessel, *RIKSENS STANDER'S*, and was lost on the east side of Pratas Shoals on September 4. The island (Pratas) bore a west-north-west direction. The vessel had a cargo of 200,000 silver pesos on board. With the help of a boat quickly dispatched from the *RIKSENS STANDER'S*, all of the cargo was saved.

18. **1800** – *EARL TALBOT*, English East Indiaman of 1,200 tons, foundered in the South China Sea during a typhoon (possibly on Pratas Shoal) while attempting to reach China via the Eastern Passage. It was the vessel's second voyage.

19. **1842** – *SINGULAR*, Spanish brig, was lost off Dongsha Qundao (Pratas) while on route from Manila to China. Vessel was said to have had gold to the value of US$50,000 on board.

20 **1845** – *CITY OF SHIREZ*, ship which struck on a reef on Dongsha Qundao (Pratas) during its voyage from Huang-pu (China) to Bombay (India). There was a salvage attempt in 1846 but the results are unclear.

21. **1852** – *CHARLOTTE*, American ship, 850 tons, Captain James Lyster, laden with cotton from Madras to Canton, was lost on Pratas Shoals at 2 a.m. on September 17. The crew was saved.

22. **1852** – *REYNARD*, steam ship (unknown origin), Captain Cracroft, lost on Pratas Shoals in 1852.

23. **1854** – *COUNTESS OF SEAFIELD*, English ship, Captain Innes, sailing on March 21 with about 750 tons of tea, silk and wool from Shanghai to London, was lost on Pratas Shoals at about 9 p.m. The crew survived.

24. **1854** – *LIVING AGE*, American clipper ship, 727 tons, sailing from Shanghai to New York and was wrecked on Pratas Shoals on December 31, 1854. The ship was laden with a full cargo of tea and silk. The crew were saved.

25. **1855** – *TOM BOWLINE*, English ship, from Chowfou, lost on Pratas Shoals in January, laden with tea. The second mate and three men were killed by pirates when in the ship's boats.

26. **1855** – *JOHANNE*, Dutch barque, Captain Bik, left Manilla on October 19 bound for Shanghai (China). On November 6, the ship struck on the northeast side of Pratas Shoal. It was impossible to get the vessel off as she immediately took in water. The following day, the crew embarked in three boats. Twenty-four hours later, they were picked up by the English barque, *ABBOTSFORD*, and arrived safely in Singapore on November 26.

27. **1856** – *MERMAID*, American ship, Captain Smith, from Bombay with a cargo of cotton, was wrecked on the night of March 2 on the north side of Pratas Shoals, having been carried on the shoal by the current.

Whilst they were trying to save the cargo, pirates set the vessel on fire. Captain Smith also reported having been told by the pirates that two other vessels, one Peruvian and one Dutch, had been lost there a short time before.

28. **1856** – *JOVEN IDHAP*, Portuguese barque, laden with rice sailing from Manilla to Macau, wrecked on Pratas Shoals in January. Two men died in their long boats.

29. **1858** – *COURSER*, American clipper ship, lost on Pratas Shoals on April 4. Captain Cole and the crew survival.

30. **1860** – *NORTH STAR* (origin unspecified), wrecked on Pratas Shoals.

31. **1862** – *PHANTOM*, American clipper ship of 1,147 tons, Captain Sargent, was lost on Pratas Shoals on July 14. She was carrying £2,000,000 in gold from California and was on a voyage from San Francisco to Hong Kong. The survivors were rescued by the *PRUTH* and arrived at Hong Kong on July 22, bringing with them the amount of $55,000 in treasure saved. The remainder was lost with the vessel. Some accounts say that Captain Sargent was drowned.

32. **1862** – *MALACCA*, Hamburg vessel, Captain Stelljes, lost on Pratas Shoals while bound for New York. The crew were picked up on the Hamburg ship, *SUSANNAH*, Captain Russ, bound to Singapore.

33. **1863** – *GEORGE SAND*, Hamburg barque, was on a voyage from San Francisco to Hong Kong when it wrecked on Pratas Shoals during a heavy typhoon on July 17. The crew and passengers reached Hong Kong on July 27 via the *KENNINGTON*. The wreck was said to have carried a cargo of £2,600,000 in California gold.

34. **1869** – *CHIEFTAIN* (origin unspecified), on voyage from Shanghai to London, lost on Pratas Shoals and the crew were saved. The cargo was looted by Chinese pirates.

35. **Year unspecified** *DOROTHEA*, (origin unspecified), while sailing from Macau to Batavia, was wrecked on Pratas Shoals.

Spratly Islands

The geographical position of the Spratly Island group is between latitude 4 degrees and 11 degrees 30 minutes north, and longitude 109 degrees 30 minutes and 117 degrees 50 minutes east. This group, which contains 100 or more islands including reefs and coral cays, is scattered over a vast oval-shaped area with a maximum diameter of about 1,000 km. The Spratlys comprise 12 regions with islands, reefs and cays.

The Spratly Islands are claimed by the following countries: People's Republic of

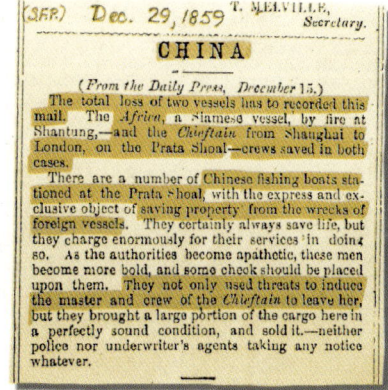

(3FR) Dec. 29, 1859   T. MELVILLE, Secretary.

CHINA

(*From the Daily Press, December 15.*)
The total loss of two vessels has to recorded this mail. The *Afrisu*, a Siamese vessel, by fire at Shantung,—and the *Chieftain* from Shanghai to London, on the Prata Shoal—crews saved in both cases.

There are a number of Chinese fishing boats stationed at the Prata Shoal, with the express and exclusive object of saving property from the wrecks of foreign vessels. They certainly always save life, but they charge enormously for their services in doing so. As the authorities become apathetic, these men become more bold, and some check should be placed upon them. They not only used threats to induce the master and crew of the *Chieftain* to leave her, but they brought a large portion of the cargo here in a perfectly sound condition, and sold it.—neither police nor underwriter's agents taking any notice whatever.

The Singapore Free Press reports the loss of the CHIEFTAIN *on Pratas Shoal.*

China, Republic of China (Taiwan), the Philippines and the Republic of Vietnam, Thailand and Malaysia. Seven of the 20 islands, islets, reefs and cays are in Vietnamese hands: Nam yit (Tizard Bank), the main base, Cay du N.E. (North Danger), Truong Sa (Spratly Island), Sin Cowe (Union Banks and reef), Sin Ton, Sandcay and Song Tu Tay. Three to four other islets are occupied by the Philippines, among them Thitu Island (the main base) and Nan Shan Island. The island of Itu Aba has for some time been used as a naval base by Taiwan.

36. **1864** – *MADRAS*, English ship of 600 tons burthen, Captain Nabb, was wrecked at 11 p.m. on February 11 on a reef situated at latitude 8 degrees 17 minutes north, longitude 111 degrees 14 minutes east. The vessel was laden with rice and on a voyage from Bangkok to Hong Kong. The crew consisting of 19 persons embarked in three boats and reached Saigon on February 20.

Other parts of the South China Sea

37. **1518** – *SANTO ANDRE*, Portuguese East Indiaman of 70 tons, under the command of Martim Guedes, was lost in the South China Sea in October while returning to Malacca from China.

38. **1605** – Spanish ship (name unknown), was lost in the South China Sea while on route to Japan. She had on board 50,000 gold crusados.

39. **1607** – *MAURITIUS*, VOC ship of 700 tons (captain unknown), arrived in the Indies (Bantam) on December 27, 1607. During a voyage from Bantam to Patani to take over the cargo of a Portuguese prizeship, the ship was lost.

40. **1653** – *SMIENT*, Dutch East Indiaman of 400 tons, Captain Thijs Krab, was wrecked while sailing from Batavia to Taiwan in June.

41. **1659** – *GLEEMUIDEN*, Dutch East Indiaman of 202 tons, was wrecked while sailing on a voyage (from Batavia) to Canton, China.

42. **1659** – *ZWARTE BUL*, VOC ship of 400 tons that was lost in the South China Sea during its voyage from Batavia to Japan.

43. **1661** – *KORTENHOEF*, Dutch East Indiaman of 216 tons, Captain Luit Pieters, was wrecked on September 16 on its way to Formosa.

44. **1663** – *WAPEN VAN ZEELAND*, Dutch East Indiaman (tonnage and captain unknown), was wrecked on a voyage to China (from Batavia?) on September 16.

45. **1663** – *S'GRAVELAND*, VOC ship, Captain Andries Pieters, while returning from Nagasaki (Japan) to Batavia (Java), the ship was wrecked.

46. **1670** – *KANEELBOOM*, Dutch East Indiaman of 300 tons, (captain unknown), was wrecked on a voyage between Bengal (India) and Batavia on November 18.

47. **1670** – *HOOGKARSPEL*, Dutch East Indiaman of 212 tons, Captain Meindert Roelofsz, was wrecked on a voyage between Tonking (North Vietnam) and Japan.

48. **1689** – *WAVEREN*, Dutch East Indiaman of 488 tons, Captain Reinier de Groot, was on a voyage from Bengal (India) to Batavia (Java), when a fire broke out in the galley on December 20 and destroyed the ship.

49. **1690** – *CANTON*, Dutch East Indiaman of 1,150 tons, Captain Dirk Peek, was on a voyage from Batavia to China and was wrecked in the South China Sea during or shortly after the year 1690.

50. **1708** – *MONSTER*, Dutch East Indiaman of 572 tons, Captain Jan Walburg, departed (from Batavia) for Japan on June 30 and was lost.

51. **1718 or 1719** – *SLOT VAN KAPELLE*, VOC ship of 600 tons, Captain Pieter van Heel, was wrecked while sailing on a voyage from Batavia to Japan during the year 1718 or 1719.

52. **1719** – *CATHARINA*, Dutch East Indiaman of 800 tons, Captain Lambert Bot, was lost on a voyage from Batavia to Japan on August 14.

53. **1724** – *APPOLLONIA*, VOC ship of 800 tons, Captain Gerbrand Mamus, was lost on a voyage from Batavia to Japan.

54. **1731** – *KNAPENBURG*, Dutch East Indiaman of 900 tons, Captain Pieter Tinnekens, was lost at sea during its voyage to Japan.

55. **1748** – *HUIS TE PERSIJN*, Dutch East Indiaman of 850 tons, Captain Dirk Bolk, was wrecked on a voyage from Japan to Batavia.

56. **1766** – *LINDENHOF*, Dutch East Indiaman of 1,150 tons, Captain Hans Bruns, was sailing from Batavia to China and was struck by lightning and exploded.

57. **1768** – *VREDENHOF*, Dutch East Indiaman of 1,150 tons, Captain Aldert Aldertsz, was sailing on a voyage (from Batavia?) to Japan and wrecked along the route.

58. **1768** – China junk, bound from Manilla to China with 360,000 dollars on board and was lost. Part of the money was probably saved.

59. **1770** – *GANZENHOEF*, Dutch East Indiaman of 880 tons, Captain Gerrit de Waal, was wrecked during a voyage from Japan to Batavia.

60. **1772** – *RIJNSBURG*, Dutch East Indiaman of 850 tons, Captain Roelof Schot, departed Batavia on July 2, 1771 bound for China but was wrecked enroute.

61. **1788** – *ADMIRAAL DE SUFFEREN*, Dutch East Indiaman of 1,300 tons, departed China on March 1 for the Netherlands, but was wrecked somewhere in the South China Sea. She was laden with Chinese porcelain. Cargo was valued at 1,008,000 florins.

62. **1788** – *MIDDELWIJK*, Dutch East Indiaman of 880 tons, Captain Kornelis de Klerk, was sailing on a voyage from Batavia to China and was wrecked.

63. **1802** – *NAUTILUS*, ship of Calcutta, was lost in September during a typhoon along with a Spanish vessel (name unknown) near the Lema Isles.

64. **1809** – *TRUE BRITON*, EIC ship of 1,198 tons, Captain George Bonham, parted company from the Bombay-bound ships in her company shortly

after leaving China and perished totally with her crew during a typhoon on October 13. This occurred at latitude 19 degrees north, longitude 115 degrees east. It was the vessel's eighth voyage.

65.   **1810** – *OCEAN*, English East Indiaman of 1,200 tons (captain unknown), sailed from Portsmouth, England on January 21, 1810. The ship was lost in the South China Seas on September 5 during a typhoon. There were no survivors. It was the ship's fifth voyage.

66.   **1833** – *NEW JERSEY*, American vessel, in the course of its voyage from Gibraltar to Canton with a valuable cargo of Spanish silver dollars, quicksilver (mercury) and lead, the ship was wrecked in November upon the Louisa Shoal in the South China Sea. The captain and crew afterwards safely made their way to Singapore in the ship's longboat.

In the early 1834, three vessels with divers departed Singapore for Louisa Shoal in hopes of recovering some of the New Jersey's lost treasure. During the salvage attempt, one of the salvage vessels, *RELIANCE*, was lost upon the shoal during a storm. The other salvage ship, *MADELINE*, returned to Singapore having successfully recovered quicksilver and lead valued at between 24,000 to 25,000 Spanish dollars. The other salvage vessel, *LUCILE*, later returned to Singapore having recovered property from the wreck to the value of 7,200 Spanish dollars.

One of the divers was drowned while attempting to salvage some quicksilver. Not all of the treasure and quicksilver was salvaged.

67.   **1836** – *HARMOODY*, English (?) vessel, departed Bombay harbour in June with a group of other ships. They were bound for China. In the South China Sea, they encountered a typhoon which caused the *HARMOODY* and the *HORMUSJEE BOMANJEE* to collide. Both vessels foundered as a result of this collision and many lives were lost (see below).

68.   **1836** – *HORMUSJEE BOMANJEE*, Parsee Company Indian vessel of 757 tons, departed Bombay harbour in June with a group of other EIC ships bound for China. In the China seas, they encountered a typhoon which caused the *HARMOODY* and the *HORMUSJEE BOMANJEE* to collide. Both vessels foundered as a result of this collision and many lives were lost (see above).

69.   **1840** – *GOLONDA*, Parsee Company ship out of India, was conveying troops on a voyage from Madras to China and foundered in a cyclone. Between 600 and 700 people perished with the ship.

70.   **1848** – *RAINBOW*, American clipper ship of 750 tons, simply vanished at sea during this year.

71.   **1851** – *HO HING KONGSOO NAKODA WON HAH YOU*, a China junk of several hundred tons, was on a voyage from Macau to Singapore and was totally lost off Calantan on December 27. Of a crew of 316 persons, 62 perished with the vessel. The entire cargo was also lost.

72.   **During or after 1855** – *COREA*, P&O Company steamship, departed

from Hong Kong with two other vessels. The barometer gave no warning but shortly thereafter, a very violent typhoon blew up. The COREA and one other ship (name not mentioned) were never seen again. There were no survivors.

73. **1872** – ARIEL, British tea clipper of 853 tons, vanished at sea during this year.

74. **1877** – CHAMPION OF THE SEAS, a privately-owned clipper ship of 1,947 tons, foundered at sea.

75. **1895** – SIR LANCELOT, British tea clipper ship of 886 tons, foundered at sea.

76. **Year unknown** – MEMNON, American clipper ship, struck on a reef in the China Sea and was lost.

THAILAND

Thailand shares its borders with Myanmar, Laos and Cambodia. Its heart is the Chao Phraya River that flows across the central plain extending from the Gulf of Siam to the foothills of the northern mountains. Total area is 513,120 sq. km (198,116 sq. miles). Thailand has over 1,200 km (700 miles) of coastline along the Gulf of Siam. Thailand was known as Siam until 1939.

1. **1851** – ARDASEER, British trading vessel, sank on April 17th at approximately latitude 9 degrees north, longitude 97 degrees 30 minutes east during its voyage from China to Singapore and Calcutta (India). Some treasure was removed before the vessel sank.

2. **1856** – NEPTUNE, ship of 1,000 tons of unknown origin, blew up on February 26th and caught fire for 28 hours before sinking off of Barat Menam (Thailand). The ship was supposed to have had a cargo of gold bars, gold leaf and sycee silver on board.

TAIWAN

Taiwan island's center is located at approximately latitude 23 degrees 30 minutes north, longitude 120 degrees 35 minutes east. In addition to the main Taiwan island, some islands off mainland China fall under Taiwan's control – Quemoy (Jinmen) and Matsu (Mazu). Total land area is 36,000 sq. km. (13,900 sq. miles). Taiwan was formerly known as Formosa and also as Zeelandia by the Dutch who established a fort there in the early 1600s.

1. **1583** – Spanish trading ship (name unknown), Captain Alonso Sanchez, was returning from Amoy (China) to Manilla (Philippines), loaded with silks, spices and gold. The ship was wrecked off the southwest coast of Taiwan. There is no record of this cargo being salvaged.

‡   **1583** – Spanish ship which sank off Taiwan while on route from China to Manila. P. Alonso Sanchez was on board. The vessel was reported to have had porcelain on board.

2.   **1622** – *SANTA CROIX*, VOC ship which was lost between Japan and P'eng-hu Lieh-tao (Taiwan) while voyaging from Japan to Taiwan.

3.   **1633** – *BROWERSHAVEN*, VOC ship of 200 tons, Captain Willem Jakobsz, arrived in the Indies (Batavia) on June 20, 1627. The ship remained in the Indies until six years later when on June 28, the ship ran aground and was destroyed by fire on the coast on Formosa.

4.   **1637** – *ZWAAN*, Dutch East Indiaman of 200 tons, Captain Adriaan Waaghals, arrived in the Indies (Batavia) on June 10, 1634. The ship stayed in the Indies and three years later on February 26, it was wrecked in the Pescadores.

5.   **1639** – *AEMILIA*, Dutch East Indiaman of 600 tons, Captain Joost Salters, arrived in the Indies (Batavia) on October 24, 1638. The following year on June 21, the ship ran ashore at Taiwan.

6.   **1639** – Spanish junk (name unknown), was on its way to its base at Santiago Bay (located on the north tip of Formosa), named Puerto de los Espanoles. It was carrying silver money for trade and the garrison's payroll. It floundered in the sea off the west coast. The treasure was too deep to be salvaged.

7.   **1639** – *ZON*, Dutch East Indiaman of 200 tons (captain unknown), arrived in the Indies (Batavia) on July 9, 1638. The ship remained in the Indies and was lost in the Pescadores on December 31, 1639.

8.   **1643** – *HERT*, Dutch East Indiaman of 200 tons (captain unknown), arrived in the Indies (Batavia) on June 17, 1639. The ship stayed in the Indies and four years later was wrecked in the Pescadores.

9.   **1644** – *ZWAAN*, Dutch East Indiaman (tonnage and captain unknown), arrived in the Indies (Batavia) on April 17, 1643. The next year on October 27, the ship was wrecked in the Pescadores. The crew, except for one man, and the cargo were saved.

10. **1654** – *TAIWAN*, VOC ship of 300 tons (captain unknown), arrived in the Indies (Batavia) on May 11, 1651. The ship remained in the Indies and three years later was wrecked near Taiwan on August 9. The crew and cargo were saved.

11. **1660** – *HARP*, Dutch East Indiaman (tonnage and captain unknown), arrived in the Indies (Batavia) on 24 February, 1659. It was wrecked the following year on June 25 (off Taiwan?).

12. **1661** – *HECTOR*, VOC ship of 600 tons, Captain Lukas Brouwersz, which along with three other Dutch East Indiamen, *S'GRAVENLAND*, *VINK* and *MARIA*, led an attack at dawn on April 30th against the Chinese at Lakjemeuse Cannal (Taiwan) to try and capture Fort Zeelandia. The Chinese fleet consisted of 60 well armed vessels, each armed with at least two guns. The *HECTOR* soon sank several of the largest junks, but the Chinese managed to surround the vessel and

grappel it. Having five or six junks alongside, the HECTOR along with the junks exploded. When the smoke cleared, nothing of the China junks or the HECTOR remained above the surface. More than a few hundred souls had perished with the ships.

13.   **1661** – *KORTENHOEF*, Dutch East Indiaman of 216 tons, Captain Luit Pieters, arrived in the Indies (Batavia) on June 20, 1659. Two years later while attempting to relieve Fort Zeelandia at Formosa, the ship was wrecked on September 16.

14.   **1661** – *KOUDERKERKE*, Dutch East Indiaman of 200 tons (captain unknown), arrived in the Indies (Batavia) on June 17, 1655. Five years later on September 19, the ship was blown up in a battle against the Chinese off Formosa.

15.   **1661** – *IMMENHORN*, Dutch East Indiaman (tonnage unknown), Captain Dirk Dirksz Jonas, arrived in the Indies (Batavia) on June 2, 1659. Two years later during a battle against the Chinese, the ship was wrecked.

16.   **1672** – *CUYLENBURGH*, Dutch East Indiaman of 468 tons, bound from Tywan (Taiwan) to Japan, and was wrecked near Kelang (a garrison belonging to the King on the north coast of Tywan). Her cargo of 210,000 florins worth of goods was lost with the ship. Some of the crew were drowned and the remainder escaped in their boats to Japan.

VIETNAM

The Vietnam region was the original core of the Annamite empire which came into being after the revolt against Chinese rule in A.D. 939. South Vietnam was formerly known as Cochin China, Central Vietnam as Annam and North Vietnam as Tongking. Its total land area is 331,689 sq. km. (128,065 sq. miles) which includes over 1,100 miles of coastline with numerous offshore islands and reefs. In the south, the coastal plains open out into the great delta of the Mekong, the world's 10th largest river.

1.   **1617** – *NUESTRA SENORA DE LORETO*, Spanish galleon that was lost off the coast of northern Vietnam (Bay of Tongking).

2.   **1633** – *KEMPAHAAN*, Dutch East Indiaman of 100 tons, Captain Kornelis Hendriksz Denijs, departed Galle (Ceylon) on December 17, 1632 and ran ashore at Cochin China on October 22.

3.   **1635** – *GROOTBROEK*, VOC ship of 240 tons (captain unknown), arrived in the Indies (Batavia) on April 28, 1631. Four years later during a voyage, the ship was captured by a Portuguese yacht and wrecked on the coast of Cochin China.

4.   **1636** – *KEIZERIN*, VOC ship of 200 tons which was lost on October 29th in the Bay of Padaran (off the coast of Champa, north Vietnam) during its voyage from Taiwan to Vietnam. Cargo was said to have

consisted of porcelain. Recent attempts to locate to the wreck have been unsuccessful.

5. **1674** – *GOUDEN LEEUW*, VOC ship of 330 tons, which arrived in the Indies (Batavia) on June 18, 1666. Eight years later, the vessel was wrecked at one of the Tiger Islands (Gulf of Tonkin ?).

6. **1683** – *IMYRNASTE*, EIC ship that was lost on February 25th on the Bar of Tongking, near Haipong (north Vietnam) during its voyage from England to China.

7. **1719** – *NUESTRA SENORA DE LORETO*, Spanish *Capitana* of an Armada commanded by General Francisco de Echeveste. The vessel was bringing several merchants to Siam and struck on a reef and sank somewhere along the coast of Tonkin. The crew were rescued by boats from the other ships but several chests of treasure were lost.

8. **1850** – A pirate Vietnamese ship under the command of Shap'ng Tsai was lost in the Gulf of Tongking. The ship supposedly had treasure on board.

9. **1864** – *FLORA*, French ship, from Marseilles bound to Saigon was lost on the Cambodian Banks, near the mouth of the river called Cua Dai on February 12. The crew were saved.

10. **Year unknown** – *BRITTO SHOAL*, which according to a book of sailing directions written in 1843, was named after a Portuguese captain who was shipwrecked there.

An old anchor salvaged from Singapore's harbour which is now on display at the Maritime Museum, Singapore.

BIBLIOGRAPHY

Books

Bowen, Frank C. *From Carrack to Clipper, A Book of Sailing Ship Models*. New York: Halton and Company, 1948

Boxer, C.R. *Dutch Merchants and Mariners in Asia, 1602–1795*. London: Variorum reprints, 1988

Boxer, C.R. *The Dutch Seaborne Empire, 1600–1800*. London: Penguin Books, 1965

Boxer, C.R. *Portuguese Conquest and Commerce in Southern Asia, 1500–1750*. London: Variorum reprints, 1985

Broeze, Frank. *Brides of the Sea, Port Cities of Asia from the 16th–20th Centuries*. Australia: New South Wales University Press, 1989

Brown, Roxanna M. *The Ceramics of Southeast Asia, Their Dating and Identification*. Singapore: Oxford University Press, 1977

Bruijn, J.R. *Dutch-Asiatic Shipping in the 17th and 18th centuries*. The Hague: Martinus Nijhoff, 1979

Chatterton, Edward Kebel. *The Old East Indiamen*. London: T. Werner Laurie Ltd, 1914

Chin, Kok Koun. *History of Southeast Asia*. Singapore: Oxford University Press, 1994

Coates, W.H. *The Old Country Trade of the East Indies*. London: Imray, Laurie, Noric and Wilson, 1911

Cotton, Sir Charles. *East Indiamen, The East India Company's Maritime Service*. London: The Batchworth Press, 1949

Cutter, Carl. *Greyhounds of the Sea*. Annapolis, Maryland: US Naval Institute, 1930

Daggett, Charles and Shaffer, Christopher. *Diving for the Griffin*. London: Weidenfield and Nicholson, 1990

De Zuniga, Martinez. *Historical View of the Phillippine Islands*. London: T. Davidson, 1814

Earle, T.F. and Villiers, John. *Albuquerque, Caesar of the East*. England: Aris and Phillips-Warminster, 1990

Elmore, H.M. *The British Mariners Directory and Guide to the Trade and Navigation of the Indian and China Seas*. Glasgow: T. Bensley, 1802

Frey, Albert Romer. *American Journal of Numistics (1916)*. New York: American Numistic Society, 1917

Haellquist, Karel Reinhold. *Asian Trade Routes, Continental and Maritime.* Curzon Press, 1991.

Heinzig, Dieter. *Disputed Islands in the South China Sea.* Hamburg: Otto Harrassowitz/Weisbaden, 1976

Horsburgh, James. *India Directory.* London: William H. Allen, 1843

Howarth, David and Howarth, Stephen. *The Story of P&O.* London: Weidenfeld and Nicolson, 1986

Jorg, C.J.A. *Porcelain and the Dutch China Trade.* The Hague: Martinus Nijhoff, 1982

Knight, Frank. *The Clipper Ship.* London: Collins, 1973

Koninckx, Christian. *The First and Second Charters of the Swedish East India Company (1731–1766).* Belgium: Van Ghemmert Publishing, 1980

Lubbock, Basil. *The Colonial Clippers.* Glasgow, 1948

Lubbock, Basil. *Coolie Ships and Oil Sailers.* London: Brown, Son and Ferguson, Nautical Publishers, 1955

MacGregor, David R. *The Tea Clippers, Their History and Development, 1833–1875.* London: Conway Maritime Press and Lloyd's of London Press, 1973

Marshall, Michael W. *Ocean Traders, From the Portuguese Discoveries to the Present Day.* New York: Facts on File, 1990

Marx, Robert F. *The Underwater Dig.* Texas: Pisces Books, 1990

Marx, Robert F. *Sunken Treasure – How to Find it.* Texas: Ram Books, 1990

Morse, Horsea Ballou. *The Chronicles of the East India Company Trading to China, 1635–1834.* London: Oxford Claredon Press, 1926

Parkinson, Northcote. *Trade in the Eastern Seas, 1793–1813.* London: Cambridge University Press, 1937

Penrose, Boies. *Sea Fights in the East Indies in the years 1602–1636.* Massachusetts: Harvard University Press, 1931

Philip's World Handbook, Country by Country. London: George Philip Ltd, 1993

Pickford, Nigel. *Atlas of Shipwreck Treasure.* London: Dorling Kindersley, 1994

Potter Jr., John S. *The Treasure Diver's Guide*. Florida: Doubleday, 1960

Schury, William Lytle. *The Manilla Galleon*. New York: E.P. Dutton and Company, 1939

Sheaf, Colin and Kilburn, Richard. *The Hatcher Porcelain Cargoes*. Oxford: Phaidon/ Christie's, 1988

Smits, H.D.A. *Sailing Instructions for the Banca Straits*. Singapore, 1847

Sutton, Jean. *Lords Of The East, The East India Company's Trading and its Ships*. Conway Maritime Press Ltd

The World of Learning 1993. England: Europa Publications Limited, 1993

Volker, T. *The Japanese Porcelain Trade of the Dutch East India Company After 1683*. Leiden: E.J. Brill, 1959

Volker, T. *Porcelain and the Dutch East India Company, 1602–1682*. Leiden: E.J. Brill, 1954

Wilkins, Harold T. *Treasure Hunting*. New Mexico: Rio Grande Press, 1939

Wilson, Derek. *The World Atlas of Treasure*. London: Pan Books, 1981

Wilson, Elizabeth. *A Guide to Oriental Ceramics*. Rutland: Charles E. Tuttle Company, 1991

Wilson, S.J. *Doits to Ducatons, The Coins of the Dutch East India Company Ship* BATAVIA. Australia: Western Australian Museum, 1989

Periodicals

Journal of the Malayan Branch of the Royal Asiatic Society (JMBRAS)

Singapore Chronicle and Commercial Register

Singapore Free Press and *Merchantile Advertiser*

Singapore Straits Times

The Legendary Kijang (Bank Negara Malaysia)

Treasure Magazine

SHIP INDEX

Ship	Nationality	Year lost	Region lost	Page no.
AAGTEKERK	VOC	1650	Indonesia	97
AARDENBURG	VOC	1685	Indonesia	98
ADMIRAAL DE SUFFEREN	VOC	1788	South China Sea	137
AEMILIA	VOC	1639	Taiwan	140
AEOLUS KLEINE	VOC	1616	Indonesia	109
AGATHA MARIA	Dutch	1861	Indonesia	104
ALBLASSERDAM	VOC	1735	China	86
ALCESTE	HMS	1817	Indonesia	95
ALEXANDER	?	1836	Malaysia	117
ALICE	?	1817	Indonesia	111
ALIOZA DE CARAVAILLA	PEI	1606	Malaysia	115
ALMIRANTA	Spanish	1598	China	85
AMELIA	Portuguese	1816	Indonesia	98
ANDREW JACKSON	American	1868	Indonesia	97
ANKEVEEN	VOC	1663	China	86
ANNA	?	?	Malaysia	117
ANNA ELISABETH	Dutch	1857	Malaysia	117
ANTARTIC	British	1857	Malaysia	117
ANTELOPE	American	1858	South China Sea	130
ANTELOPE PACKET	EIC	1783	New Guinea	120
APPOLLONIA	VOC	1724	South China Sea	137
AREND	VOC	1610	Philippines	122
ARIEL	English	1872	South China Sea	139
ARIENIS	English	1852	Indonesia	111
ART VAN NES	Dutch	1854	New Guinea	120
ARDASEER	British	1851	Thailand	139
ARION	VOC	1714	South China Sea	129
ARTEMISIA	English	1854	Indonesia	105
ARU	PEI	bfr 1599	Indonesia	91
ASIA	?	1827	Philippines	126
ASIA	EIC	1809	Bangladesh	83
ATHENA	English	1815	India	88
AVA	British	1879	Bangladesh	84
BAMBEEK	VOC	1702	Malaysia	36, 116
BANGALORE	?	1802	Indonesia	99
BANTAM	VOC	1627	Indonesia	101
BATAVIA	VOC	1629	Australia	28
BERENICE	British	1853	Indonesia	95
BEVERWIJK	VOC	1631	Indonesia	85
BERGEN OP ZOOM	VOC	1650	Indonesia	98
BLACK LION	EIC	1618	Indonesia	101
BLACK SWAN	Dutch	1858	New Guinea	120
BODE	VOC	1684	Indonesia	102
BORNHOLM	?	?	Malaysia	116
BRAK	VOC	1648	Bangladesh	82

Ship	Nationality	Year lost	Region lost	Page no.
BREEDAM	VOC	1633	Indonesia	101
BRITAIN'S QUEEN	English	1857	Indonesia	96
BRITTO SHOAL	?	?	Vietnam	142
BROKEKERHAVEN	VOC	1633	China	85
BRONSTEDE	VOC	1697	Indonesia	102
BROWERSHAVEN	VOC	1633	Taiwan	140
BRUINVIS	VOC	1658	Philippines	124
BUEN JESUS	Spanish	1643	Philippines	123
BUSSORAH	India	1862	Singapore	129
CALCUTTA	English	1799	Malaysia	116
CALCUTTA	English	1860	Myanmar	119
CALEDONIA	French	1857	Singapore	128
CANTON	VOC	1690	South China Sea	137
CAPITANA	Spanish	1598	China	85
CAPITANA	Spanish	1756	Philippines	125
CAPITANA DE ESPANA	Spanish	1637	Philippines	123
CAPTAIN BURNEY	India	1842	Malaysia	117
CAROLINE	English	1816	Malaysia	117
CASTLE HUNTLEY	English	1853	South China Sea	130
CATHARINA	VOC	1719	South China Sea	137
CATHERINE	EIC	1716	Indonesia	111
CELEBES	English	1863	Indonesia	106
CHAMPAN	Spanish	1639	Philippines	123
CHAMPION OF THE SEAS	?	1877	South China Sea	139
CHARLES FORBES	?	1858	Malaysia	118
CHARLES HENRY	Belgian	1863	Indonesia	96
CHARLOTTE	American	1852	South China Sea	134
CHIEFTAN	?	1869	South China Sea	135
CHINA	VOC	1608	Indonesia	112
CHINA	English	1856	Indonesia	104
CHINA PACKET	American	1868	Philippines	127
CITY OF SHIREZ	?	1845	South China Sea	134
COLUMBIAN	American	1824	Indonesia	95
COLUMBIAN	?	1845	Indonesia	37, 95
CONCEICAO	PIE	1620	Malaysia	116
COREA	English	1855	South China Sea	138
CORNELIUS HAJA	Dutch	1850	Indonesia	95
CORNELLA	?	1858	Bangladesh	83
COROMANDEL	English	after 1797	Indonesia	97
COUNTESS OF LONDON	English	1816	Philippines	126
COUNTESS OF SEAFIELD	English	1854	South China Sea	134
COURSER	American	1858	South China Sea	135
CUYLENBURGH	VOC	1672	Taiwan	141
DAMIATE	VOC	1677	Indonesia	105
DE GOEDE HOOP	VOC	1633	Indonesia	92
DELFSHAVEN	VOC	1633	Indonesia	102
DELFSHAVEN	VOC	1653	Indonesia	89
DEN BRIEL	VOC	1681	Myanmar	119
DEN HELDER	VOC	1690	Bangladesh	82

Ship	Nationality	Year lost	Region lost	Page no.
DENHAM	EIC	1758	Indonesia	110
DERKINA TITIA	Dutch	1860	Indonesia	104
DIANA	English	1817	Malaysia	117
DIEMEREER	VOC	1670	Indonesia	92
DIEMEREER	VOC	1747	New Guinea	119
DOMBURG	VOC	1627	China	85
DOROTHEA	?	?	South China Sea	135
DOURO	English		South China Sea	130
DRAAK	VOC	1796	Indonesia	103
DUARTE DE GUERRA	PEI	1606	Malaysia	115
EARL OF DARTHMOUTH	EIC	1682	India	88
EARL OF DARTHMOUTH	EIC	1782	Bangladesh	83
EARL TALBOT	EIC	1800	South China Sea	134
EARL TEMPLE	British	1759	South China Sea	129
EENDRACHT	VOC	1622	Indonesia	89
ELLEN ROGER	American	?	China	87
EMMA	American	1862	South China Sea	39, 133
ENCARNACION	Spanish	1649	Philippines	123
ENKHUIZEN	VOC	1607	Indonesia	100
ENXOBREGAS	PEI	1511	Indonesia	108
ERASMUS	Portuguese	1606	Malaysia	116
ESPRITU SANTO	Manilla	1576	Philippines	120
ETHIOPIA	India	1873	Myanmar	119
EUROPA	VOC	1784	Indonesia	103
EXPEDITION	EIC	1620	Japan	114
FALMOUTH	EIC	1766	Myanmar	117
FAME	EIC	1824	Indonesia	22, 110
FERROLENA URCA	Spanish	1802	China	86
FEDELIDAD	Spanish	1821	Philippines	126
FLEINE AEOLUS	VOC	1616	Indonesia	109
FLOR DO MAR	PEI	1511	Indonesia	32, 33, 46, 54–64, 65, 107
FLORA	French	1864	Vietnam	142
FLORA TEMPLE	American	1859	South China Sea	130
FORBES	English	1806	Indonesia	94
FRANEKER	VOC	1642	Malaysia	116
FRANKFORT OLD	English	1863	Indonesia	99
FREDERIC ALDOLPHUS	SEI	1761	South China Sea	134
FREDERICK VI	British	1846	Indonesia	107
FREDERICK HENDRICK	VOC	1648	Indonesia	92
FROLIC	?	1858	Malaysia	118
GALION SAINT SYMON	PEI	1606	Malaysia	115
GANZENHOEF	VOC	1770	South China Sea	137
GEELMUIDEN	VOC	1659	China	86
GEIT	VOC	1668	Indonesia	105
GELDERMALSEN	VOC	1751	Indonesia	35, 37, 38, 107
GELE BEER	VOC	1684	Indonesia	110
GENEROUS FRIENDS	?	1801	South China Sea	129
GEORGE SAND	Germany	1863	South China Sea	134

Ship	Nationality	Year lost	Region lost	Page no.
GIESSENBERG	VOC	1766	Indonesia	90
GLASS WRECK	?	?	Indonesia	31, 64, 65, 66, 79, 94
GLEEMUIDEN	VOC	1659	South China Sea	136
GOEDE HOOP	VOC	1654	Indonesia	89
GOES	VOC	1651	China	86
GOLONDA	India	1840	South China Sea	138
GONDOLIER	English	1845	Indonesia	95
GOOILAND	VOC	1682	Indonesia	110
GOUDEN LEEUW	VOC	1634	Borneo	84
GOUDEN LEEUW	VOC	1674	Vietnam	142
GRACEDIEU	EIC	1698	Bangladesh	82
GRIFFION	VOC	1625	Indonesia	106
GRIFFIOEN	VOC	1663	Indonesia	102
GRIFFIN	EIC	1761	Philippines	125
GROOTBROEK	VOC	1635	Vietnam	141
GROET AEOLUS	VOC	1617	Philippines	122
GROTE ZON	VOC	1617	Philippines	122
HAPPY ENTRANCE	EIC	1670	Bangladesh	82
HARING	VOC	1656	Indonesia	89
HARLEQUIN	?	1845	Bangladesh	83
HATCHER JUNK	China	?	South China Sea	36
HARMOODY	English	1836	South China Sea	138
HARP	VOC	1660	Taiwan	140
HECTOR	EIC	1617	Indonesia	101
HECTOR	VOC	1661	Taiwan	140
HENDRIK FREDERIK	VOC	1601	Indonesia	106
HENDRIK WESTER	Dutch	1854	Indonesia	95
HERT	VOC	1643	Taiwan	140
HERTOG VAN BRUNSWIJK	VOC	1795/96	Indonesia	103
HINCHINBROOKE	EIC	1781	Bangladesh	83
HOFWEGEN	VOC	1748	Indonesia	103
HO HING KONGSOO NAKODA WON HAH YOU	China	1851	South China Sea	138
HONSELAARSDIJK	VOC	1698	Indonesia	102
HOOGKARSPEL	VOC	1670	South China Sea	136
HOORN	EIC	1619	Indonesia	109
HORMUSJEE BOMANJEE	India	1836	South China Sea	138
HOTSPUR	American	1863	South China Sea	133
HOWARD	VOC	1622	Japan	114
HUIS TE KLEEF	VOC	1684	Indonesia	102
HUIS TE NOORDWIJK	VOC	1683	Indonesia	112
HUIS TE PERSIJN	VOC	1748	South China Sea	137
HUIS TE VELSEN	VOC	1683	China	120
HUIS TE VELSEN	VOC	1682	Indonesia	112
IMMENHORN	VOC	1661	Taiwan	141
IMYRNASTE	EIC	1683	Taiwan	142
INDIAN QUEEN	?	1719	New Guinea	119
INDUS	VOC	1794	Indonesia	103

Ship	Nationality	Year lost	Region lost	Page no.
INTERPID	American	1860	Indonesia	96
ISLE O' MAY	English	1864	Indonesia	97
JACK	?	1853	New Guinea	120
JAMES AND MARY	EIC	1694	Bangladesh	82
JAMSETJEE JEEJEEBHOY	India	1836	China	87
JANET HUTTON	English	1825	Myanmar	119
JAPAN	American	1875	China	87
JESUS MARIA	Spanish	1620	Philippines	122
JOHANNA	VOC	1730	Bangladesh	82
JOHANNA MARIA	Dutch	1856	Philippines	127
JOHANNA MARIA WILHELMINA	VOC	1831	Indonesia	89
JOHANNE	Dutch	1855	South China Sea	134
JOHN BANNERMAN	English	1837	South China Sea	130
JOHN CURREY	?	1855	Malaysia	117
JONGE FRANK	VOC	1789	Indonesia	103
JONKER	VOC	1647	China	85
JONKER	VOC	1667	China	86
JOVAN IDHAP	Portuguese	1856	South China Sea	135
JUFFER	VOC	1650	Indonesia	98
JULIETTE	?	1857	Indonesia	89
KAMEEL	VOC	1630	Indonesia	92
KANEELBOOM	VOC	1670	South China Sea	136
KASTEEL VAN WOERDEN	VOC	1744	Indonesia	103
KATTENDIJK	VOC	1709	Indonesia	111
KEIZERIN	VOC	1636	Vietnam	141
KEMPHAAN	VOC	1633	Vietnam	141
KLEINE ADOLUS	VOC	1616	Indonesia	109
KLEVERSKERKE	VOC	1761	Indonesia	105
KNAPENBURG	VOC	1731	South China Sea	137
KOE	VOC	1652	China	86
KONING DAVID	VOC	1661	Myanmar	119
KORTENHOEF	VOC	1661	South China Sea	136, 141
KOUDERKERKE	VOC	1661	Taiwan	141
KROONVOGEL	VOC	1686	Indonesia	102
LACKASSAR	English	1825	China	87
LA GALERA	Spanish	1756	Philippines	125
LA PAIX	French	1805	Malaysia	115, 116
LEEUWIN	VOC	1664	Indonesia	105
LE MINERVE	French	1817	Indonesia	95
LIEUTENANT ADMIRAL STELLINGWERF	Dutch	1857	Indonesia	104
LILLO	VOC	1657	Indonesia	102
LINDENHOF	VOC	1766	South China Sea	137
LIVING AGE	American	1854	South China Sea	134
LOOSDUINEN	VOC	1672	Bangladesh	82
LORD HOLLAND	EIC	1769	Bangladesh	83
LORD LOWTHER	English	1843	Malaysia	117
LORD MANSFIELD	EIC	1773	Bangladesh	83

Ship	Nationality	Year lost	Region lost	Page no.
LUIPAARD	VOC	1650	Indonesia	98
MAAN	VOC	1622	Japan	114
MAAN	VOC	1642	Indonesia	98
MAARSSEVEEN	VOC	1748	Indonesia	99
MAASTRICHT	VOC	1642	Indonesia	89
MACASSAR	Belgian	1858	Indonesia	106
MADALENA	Spanish	1631	Philippines	123
MADRAS	English	1864	South China Sea	136
MADRO DI DIOS	PEI	1636	Malaysia	116
MAJOR	EIC	1784	Bangladesh	83
MAKREEL	VOC	1656	Indonesia	111
MALACCA	Germany	1862	South China Sea	135
MARIA	Spanish	1797	Philippines	126
MARIE THERESE	French	1872	Indonesia	54, 57, 97
MARQUIS OF CAMDEN	EIC	1817	China	87
MAURITIUS	VOC	1607	South China Sea	136
MECA NAU	Achinese	1527	Indonesia	108
MEMNON	American	1851	Indonesia	95
MEMNON	American	?	South China Sea	139
MERCURIUS	Dutch	1856	Indonesia	107
MERMAID	American	1856	South China Sea	134
MIDDELBURG	VOC	1606	Malaysia	115
MIDDELBURG	VOC	1606	Malaysia	116
MIDDELWIJK	VOC	1788	South China Sea	137
MODESTE	HMS	1802	China	87
MOERKAPELLE	VOC	1703	Indonesia	110
MONSTER	VOC	1708	South China Sea	137
MYSORE	India	1819	China	87
NASSAU	VOC	1606	Malaysia	115
NAUTILUS	VOC	1802	South China Sea	137
NEPTUNE	?	1856	Thailand	139
NEVA	French	1875	Indonesia	104
NEW JERSEY	American	1833	South China Sea	138
NICOLAS CEZARD	French	1858	Indonesia	104
NIEWE SONNE	VOC	1617	Philippines	122
NIEUWENDAM	VOC	1670	Indonesia	102
NIEWEKERK	VOC	1748	Indonesia	90
NIJMEGEN	VOC	1632	Indonesia	101
NINA	English	1873	China	87
NINA CHRISTINA	?	1617	China	85
NOORDBEEK	VOC	1730	Indonesia	90
NORTH STAR	?	1860	South China Sea	135
NOSSA SENHORA DA GRACA	PIE	1608	Japan	114
NUESTRA SENORA DE LA GUIA	Spanish	1741	Philippines	125
NUESTRA SENORA DE LA REMMDIOS	Spanish	1603	Philippines	122

Ship	Nationality	Year lost	Region lost	Page no.
NUESTRA SENORA DE LORETO	Spanish	1617	Vietnam	141
NUESTRA SENORA DE LA DOLORES	Spanish	1729	Philippines	125
NUESTRA SENORA DE VIDA	Spanish	1621	Philippines	123
NUESTRA SENORA DE LORETO	Spanish	1719	Vietnam	142
OCEAN	EIC	1796	Indonesia	99
OCEAN	EIC	1810	South China Sea	138
OEGSTGEEST	VOC	1719	Indonesia	103
OHIO	German	1852	Philippines	127
ONEIDA	American	1870	Japan	114
ONTARIO	American	1797	Indonesia	97
OOSTZANEN	VOC	1630	Indonesia	110
OSDORP	VOC	1674	Bangladesh	82
OUDERKERK	VOC	1627	China	85
OUWERKERK	VOC	1728	Indonesia	103
PACHA	English	1851	Malaysia	117
PAGADET	VOC	1677	Indonesia	105
PARSEE	British	1845	Indonesia	107
PASCOA	India	1836	Singapore	128
PEPERBAAL	VOC	1663	Japan	114
PERSIA	Indian	1864	Bangladesh	83
PESOUTON	Indian	1792	Bangladesh	83
PHANTOM	American	1862	South China Sea	135
PHEONIX	?	1855	New Guinea	120
PIJLSWAART	VOC	1765	Indonesia	103
PILAR	Spanish	1750	Philippines	125
PINANG	Singapore	1857	Singapore	128
PIONEER	American	1862	Indonesia	104
PORT CARAMEL	?	1555	Indonesia	91
PRINS WILLEM	VOC	1637	Indonesia	111
PRINS WILLEM HENDRICK	VOC	1686	Indonesia	93
QUETTA	India	1890	New Guinea	120
RAINBOW	American	1848	South China Sea	138
RAINBOW	English	1891	Philippines	127
REFUGE	EIC	1623	Indonesia	101
REGENT	EIC	1822	Philippines	126
REINDEER	American	1859	Philippines	127
RELIANCE	?	1834	South China Sea	138
RESISTANCE	British	1798	Indonesia	110
REYNARD	?	1852	South China Sea	134
RIJNSBURG	VOC	1638	Philippines	123
RIJNSBURG	VOC	1772	South China Sea	137
RISDAM	VOC	1726	Malaysia	118
ROBERTUS HENDRIKUS	Dutch	1856	Indonesia	103
RODE HERT	VOC	1665	Japan	114
RODE LEEUW	VOC	1613	North China Sea	120

Ship	Nationality	Year lost	Region lost	Page no.
ROEK	VOC	1645	Indonesia	89
ROYAL CAPTAIN	EIC	1773	Philippines	126
ROYAL GEORGE	EIC	1825	China	87
RYNSBURG	VOC	1772	China	86
SACRA FAMILIA	Spanish	1730	Philippines	125
SAINT ANTONIA	Portuguese	1804	South China Sea	129
SAINT LUIS	Spanish	1598	China	85
SAMUEL RUSSEL	American	1870	Indonesia	97
SALACIA	English	1862	Indonesia	96
SAN AMBROSIO	Spanish	1639	Philippines	123
SAN ANDRES	Spanish	1798	Philippines	126
SAN ANTONIO	Spanish	1603	Philippines	122
SAN ANTONIO DE PADUA	Spanish	1679	Philippines	124
SAN CRISTOBOL	Spanish	1735	Philippines	125
SAN DIEGO	Spanish	1600	Philippines	121
SAN DIEGO	Spanish	1654	Philippines	124
SAN FELIPE	Spanish	1590	Philippines	121
SAN FELIPE	Spanish	1596	Japan	113
SAN FRANCISCO	Spanish	1608	Japan	113
SAN FRANCISCO JAVIER	Spanish	1653	Philippines	123
SAN FRANCISCO JAVIER	Spanish	1705	Philippines	124
SAN JERONIMO	Spanish	1596	Philippines	121
SAN JOSE	Spanish	1694	Philippines	124
SAN JUANILLO	Spanish	1578	Philippines	121
SAN LUIS	Spanish	1646	Philippines	123
SAN MARTIN	China	1587	China	85
SAN NICOLAS	Spanish	1620	Philippines	123
SAN PABLO	Spanish	?	Philippines	121
SAN PEDRO	Spanish	1782	Philippines	126
SAN SEBASTIAO	PEI	1565	Indonesia	109
SANTA ANA	Spanish	1620	Philippines	122
SANTA CLARA	PIE	1508	Indonesia	107
SANTA CROIX	VOC	1622	Taiwan	140
SANTA MARIA MADALENA	Spanish	1734	Philippines	125
SANTO ANDRE	PEI	1518	South China Sea	136
SANTO CHRISTO DE BURGOS	Spanish	1693	Philippines	124
SANTO CHRISTO DE BURGOS	Spanish	1726	Philippines	124
SANTO THOMAS	Spanish	1601	Philippines	121
SAO PAULO	PEI	1561	Indonesia	108
SCHAKENBOS	VOC	1752	Indonesia	89
SCHELLAG	VOC	1702	Indonesia	102
SCHERMER	VOC	1671	Indonesia	92
SCHIEDAM	VOC	1633	Indonesia	92
SEVERN	American	1802	Indonesia	37, 95
S'GRAVELAND	VOC	1663	South China Sea	136
SHAFTSBURY	?	?	Indonesia	111
SHAH MUNSHY	?	1796	Singapore	128

Ship	Nationality	Year lost	Region lost	Page no.
SIMON MAU	Portuguese	1606	Malaysia	115
SINGAPORE	British	1867	Japan	114
SINGULAR	Spanish	1842	South China Sea	134
SIR LANCELOT	English	1895	South China Sea	139
SLOT VAN KAPELLE	VOC	1718	South China Sea	137
SLOTEN	VOC	1633	China	85
SMIENT	VOC	1653	South China Sea	136
SOCOTRA	India	1882	Myanmar	119
SOUBURG	Dutch	1858	Indonesia	105
SOVEREIGN OF THE SEAS	English	1860	Malaysia	118
SPEED	English	1862/63	Indonesia	104
SPEEDWELL	Scottish	1702	Malaysia	116
SPERWER	VOC	1653	North China Sea	120
STADHUIS VAN DELFT	VOC	1731	Indonesia	112
STAFFORD	EIC	1779	Bangladesh	83
STIRLING CASTLE	?	?	Indonesia	95
STOMPNEUS	VOC	1673	Indonesia	102
SULTANA	?	1841	Philippines	127
SUN	EIC	1618	Indonesia	109
SUN	?	1826	New Guinea	120
SUSANNAH	Germany	1862	Indonesia	107
SWALLOW PACKET	EIC	1823	Bangladesh	83
SYED KHAN	?	1855	Indonesia	106
TAIWAN	VOC	1654	Taiwan	140
TELLICHERRY	India (?)	1808	Philippines	126
TER VEERE	VOC	1617	Philippines	122
THAILAND JUNK	?	?	Thailand	46, 47
THEEBOOM	VOC	1711	Indonesia	90
THOMAS	EIC	1618	Indonesia	105
THOMASINE	EIC	1617	Indonesia	105
THUNDER	?	1867	Bangladesh	83
TIJER	VOC	1650	Indonesia	98
TOM BOWLINE	English	1855	South China Sea	134
TRADES INCREASE	EIC	1611/13	Indonesia	100, 101
TRANSIT	English	1857	Indonesia	40, 96
TRAVERS	EIC	1808	Myanmar	119
TREVITORE	EIC	1678	Philippines	124
TRUE BRITON	EIC	1809	South China Sea	137
UITDAM	V.O.C.	1677	Indonesia	110
UNICORN	EIC	1619	China	85
UNION	EIC	1816	Indonesia	110
UTRECHT	VOC	1641	Indonesia	106
UTRECHT	VOC	1654	South China Sea	134
VALKENBURG	VOC	1647	Indonesia	92
VALKENISSE	VOC	1740	Indonesia	103
VANSITTART	EIC	1789	Indonesia	19, 30, 36, 93
VESTA	English	1858	Indonesia	96
VIANEN	VOC	1629	Indonesia	111
VICTORIA	Spanish	1660	Philippines	124

Ship	Nationality	Year lost	Region lost	Page no.
VISURAIS	German	1855	Indonesia	112
VLEERMUIS (GULDEN)	VOC	1655	China	86
VOETBOOG	VOC	1700	Indonesia	105
VOLLENHOVEN	VOC	1663	Japan	114
VONDELLE	Dutch	1857	South China Sea	130
VREDENBURG	VOC	1670	Malaysia	118
VREDENHOF	VOC	1768	South China Sea	137
VUNG TAO	China	?	Vietnam	23
WALCHEREN	VOC	1608	Indonesia	112
WALCHERN	VOC	1630	Indonesia	110
WALVIS	VOC	1663	Indonesia	98
WAPEN VAN ZEELAND	VOC	1663	South China Sea	136
WATERHOEN	VOC	1672	Indonesia	89
WAVEREN	VOC	1689	South China Sea	137
WENA	Dutch	1817	Indonesia	103
WENDELA	VOC	1735	Indonesia	110
WESTBROEK	VOC	1697	Indonesia	111
WESTERVERLD	VOC	1679	Bangladesh	82
WIERINGEN	VOC	1636	Malaysia	116
WILLIAM	EIC	1658	Philippines	124
WILLEM KRONPRINS	Dutch	1878	Indonesia	97
WINDHOND	VOC	1658	Indonesia	102
WITTE DUIF	VOC	1650	China	85
WYNDHAM	India	1815	China	87
YANGZEE	American	1871	South China Sea	133
ZARAH	?	1857	Singapore	128
ZEELANDIA	VOC	1619	Indonesia	110
ZEEMEEUW	VOC	1653	Indonesia	102
ZEEPLOEG	VOC	1780	Indonesia	112
ZIERIKZEE	VOC	1668	Indonesia	105
ZIJPE	VOC	1690	Indonesia	102
ZINGARI	American	1854	Indonesia	103
ZON	VOC	1639	Taiwan	140
ZWAAN	VOC	1637	Taiwan	140
ZWAAN	VOC	1644	Taiwan	140
ZWARTE BUL	VOC	1659	South China Sea	136

Shipwrecks whose names are unknown

Ship	Nationality	Year lost	Region lost	Page no.
?	PEI	1509	Malaysia	114
?	PEI	1512	Indonesia	106
?	PEI	1516	Indonesia	108
?	Portuguese	1516	Indonesia	108
?	PEI	1519	Malaysia	114
?	PEI	1523	Malaysia	114
?	Spanish	1527	Indonesia	106
?	PEI	1527	Indonesia	108
?	China	1541	China	84
?	Portuguese	1542	China	84
?	Achinese	1565	Indonesia	109
?	PEI	1571	Indonesia	106
?	PIE	1573	Japan	112
?	Achinese	1578	Singapore	127
?	Portuguese	1580	Indonesia	98
?	Portuguese	1583	India	88
?	PIE	1583	Japan	112
?	Portuguese	1583	Malaysia	115
?	Portuguese	1583	Malaysia	115
?	Portuguese	1583	Singapore	128
?	Spanish	1583	Taiwan	139
?	Spanish	1589	Philippines	121
?	Spanish	1589	Philippines	121
?	PEI	bfr 1599	Indonesia	91
?	China	1599	Japan	113
?	Portuguese	1601	Indonesia	100
?	Portuguese	1601	Indonesia	108
?	Spanish	1605	South China Sea	136
?	Dutch	1606	India	88
?	Portuguese	1608	Borneo	84
?	Spanish	1609	Japan	113
?	PEI	1609	South China Sea	133
?	EIC	1611	Indonesia	92
?	Spanish	1613	Philippines	122
?	Portuguese	1615	Malaysia	118
?	Spanish	1616/17	Japan	114
?	Acheh	1629	Malaysia	116
?	Portuguese	1636	Malaysia	116
?	Spanish	1639	Taiwan	140
?	PEI	1660	Indonesia	98
?	Portuguese	1660	Indonesia	98
?	?	1660	Indonesia	98
?	PEI	1690	South China Sea	129
?	?	1717	Malaysia	118
?	Spanish	1735	Philippines	125
?	VOC	1736	Indonesia	93

Ship	Nationality	Year lost	Region lost	Page no.
?	Spanish	1762	Philippines	126
?	China	1768	South China Sea	137
?	Portuguese	1787	Malaysia	116
?	Spanish	1797	Philippines	126
?	EIC	1799	Indonesia	94
?	?	1799	Indonesia	93
?	Portuguese	1806	Malaysia	117
?	Portuguese	1816	Indonesia	94
?	China	1830	Singapore	128
?	English	1845	Indonesia	95
?	Vietnam	1850	Vietnam	142
?	?	1854	Indonesia	96
?	Dutch	1854	New Guinea	120

Shipwrecks whose names and the year of sinking are unknown

Ship	Nationality	Year lost	Region lost	Page no.
?	American	?	Indonesia	95
?	China	?	Indonesia	95
?	Portuguese	?	Vietnam	

Picture Credits

Special thanks to the Singapore National Library (Southeast Asia Collection) who very kindly allowed their collection of antique nautical charts to be photographed and reproduced in this book – pages 107, 113, 121, 129

Our thanks also to the Port of Singapore Authority (Maritime Museum) for allowing illustrations and pictures from their collection to be reproduced – pages 10, 12, 13, 128, 142

Thanks also to Antiques of the Orient, Singapore for permission to reproduce pictures – pages 1, 22, 80

Christie's Images of Amsterdam kindly allowed the use of their pictures – pages 23, 28

Andrew Merewether kindly provided the pictures on pages 8 and 15

The Royal Netherlands Embassy are acknowledged with thanks for the loan of a picture – page 94

The Money Museum, Bank Negara gave permission to use a picture – page 17

Skin Diver magazine kindly gave permission to use the picture on page 58

All other colour pictures reproduced here were taken by the author.

ABOUT THE AUTHOR

Tony Wells became a certified scuba diver at age 14 while living in Hawaii. He graduated as a professional deep sea diver from California's Commercial Diving Center in 1980. In January 1982, he came to Singapore to pursue a commerical diving career in Asia's booming oilfield industry. Although he worked as a construction and NDT (non-destructive testing) diver offshore for many years, underwater photography was his specialty.

Throughout his diving career, Tony has explored many shipwrecks and was involved with the two year search for the lost Portuguese East Indiaman, the *FLOR DO MAR*. He also has a company based in Singapore called Searchmasters providing maritime research services, maritime archeological excavation, underwater photography, hydrographical surveys and metal detecting services.

He also volunteers his free time to assist on archaeological land digs sponsored by the Singapore National Museum. Tony is a member of the American Society for Amateur Archaeology (ASAA), an organization formed in 1993 serving both amateurs and members of the public who have a budding interest in archaeology. Hopefully, these experiences will come in handy for him on future shipwreck and salvage projects.